A WOMAN'S GUIDE TO

HEARING GOD'S VOICE

FINDING DIRECTION AND PEACE
THROUGH THE STRUGGLES OF LIFE

LEIGHANN McCOY

BETHANY HOUSE PUBLISHERS

a division of Baker Publishing Group
Minneapolis, Minnesota

© 2013 by Leighann McCoy

Published by Bethany House Publishers
11400 Hampshire Avenue South
Bloomington, Minnesota 55438
www.bethanyhouse.com

Bethany House Publishers is a division of
Baker Publishing Group, Grand Rapids, Michigan

Printed in the United States of America

Library of Congress Cataloging-in-Publication Data
McCoy, Leighann
    A woman's guide to hearing God's voice : finding direction and peace
through the stuggles of life / Leighann McCoy
        p.   cm.
    Summary: "Speaker and Bible Study leader teaches readers how to hear and understand God's voice, specifically in the midst of struggles"—Provided by publisher.
        ISBN 978-0-7642-1094-5 (pbk. : alk. paper)
        1. Christian women—Religious life. I. Title.
    BV4527.M3735 2013
    248.8′43—dc23   2013007781

Unless otherwise indicated, Scripture quotations are from the Holy Bible, New International Version®. NIV®. Copyright © 1973, 1978, 1984, 2011 by Biblica, Inc.™ Used by permission of Zondervan. All rights reserved worldwide. www.zondervan.com

Scripture quotations identified HCSB quotations are from the Holman Christian Standard Bible, copyright 1999, 2000, 2002, 2003 by Holman Bible Publishers. Used by permission.

Scripture quotations identified THE MESSAGE are from The Message by Eugene H. Peterson, copyright © 1993, 1994, 1995, 2000, 2001, 2002. Used by permission of NavPress Publishing Group. All rights reserved.

Scripture quotations identified NASB are from the New American Standard Bible®, copyright © 1960, 1962, 1963, 1968, 1971, 1972, 1973, 1975, 1977, 1995 by The Lockman Foundation. Used by permission.

Scripture quotations identified NLT are from the Holy Bible, New Living Translation, copyright © 1996, 2004, 2007 by Tyndale House Foundation. Used by permission of Tyndale House Publishers, Inc., Carol Stream, Illinois 60188. All rights reserved.

Scripture quotations identified NKJV are from the New King James Version. Copyright © 1982 by Thomas Nelson, Inc. Used by permission. All rights reserved.

All emphasis in Scripture is the author's.

Cover design by Lookout Design, Inc.
Cover photo: Dougal Waters/Image Bank/Getty Images

Author is represented by Smith Management Partners, LLC

13   14   15   16   17   18   19   7   6   5   4   3   2   1

A WOMAN'S GUIDE
TO
HEARING GOD'S VOICE

Dedicated to my granddaughter

Misty Sierra Crowe

You helped me discover that God's greatest blessings
often come through the fire—
and that I was made to be a "Nana."
Keep blooming, my beautiful desert flower.

Contents

Part 4: God Will Make a Way

Acknowledgments

Writing a book might seem like a personal task, but I have to confess that the books I write are more of a group project. Without the following people, this book would have never come to be.

First there is my good husband, best friend, and life partner, Tom McCoy. Since he's been my pastor for twenty-four years, most likely much of what I teach came first from what he preached. Not only that, but without his encouragement I would have never sent the first proposal to a publisher. He earned Husband of the Year for making good on the vows he took in 1987 to love me "in sickness and in health." I would not be who I am without him.

Then there are my three children who, just because they call me Mother, have given their lives to be living, breathing illustrations in my books. Mikel and Kaleigh even had to sign releases, and TJ got off easy this go-round because he charges me for the mention of his name. I never knew what ferocious love was until these three called me Mom. And I'm grateful for what they've taught and continue to teach me.

I have two other "children," and although they are new to me, their impact on my life and my journey with God has been tremendous. These two have maybe even had the most influence on the truths I'm sharing in this book. There is my son-in-law, Austin, who is serving today in the U.S. Army and on tour in Afghanistan. And there is my beautiful granddaughter, Misty, to whom I've dedicated this book.

I am blessed to still have my parents here on earth with me, and their encouragement during these days was precious to me. I am who I am because of what they have poured into me.

Of course I also have my "book people" to thank: my manager, Ron Smith, who chooses to believe in me; and my team at Bethany House Publishers, who make my writing better and who tell the world I've got something to say: Andy McGuire, Ellen Chalifoux, and Brett Benson. I am truly grateful to each of these and the others who make my manuscript a book.

I could not go without also thanking the family of faith we call Thompson Station Church. When God called Tom and me to the dark places, they insisted on following us there. And they brought food. Over a hundred people prepared meals for my family for eight months. They prayed for us and sent us cards, text messages, and emails to encourage us every step of the way. I am so grateful to them for their ministry of encouragement. I also want to thank our pastors and ministry assistants, especially my assistant, Rhonda Brady. She kept me on track when my chemo brain threatened to derail me.

And last but certainly not least, I want to thank some of my dearest friends and prayer partners. Not only did they pray me through this project, but they also provided homemade chicken noodle soup, grapefruit juice, and companionship along the way. Terra, Kathleen, Marti, and Karen, you know that you are dear to me!

Introduction

Recently someone asked me how I was doing. I didn't answer right away. I paused long enough to ponder whether I should tell them the truth or just give them a quick, "Fine, how are you?" with a cheery smile. In an effort to maintain my integrity and yet not be caught in a thirty-minute diatribe, I grinned and said, "I'm navigating crazy, how are you doing?"

Who isn't doing that? Who has ever lived without dealing with crazy people, crazy situations, crazy thoughts, and crazy feelings?

While this book is mostly about learning to hear and respond to the voice of God, it is also about growing in your understanding that He is the same today as He was yesterday, and He will be the same tomorrow as He is today. God never changes, nor do His promises. But sometimes the struggles of life cause us to doubt that truth. This book is about taking hold of Truth and refusing to let Him go.

A Surprise on the Battlefield

While I was writing my previous book, *Spiritual Warfare for Women*, I experienced several crises in my life. When my manager, Ron, called to tell me that Bethany House had accepted my book proposal, my plane had just landed on a runway in Las Vegas. I was there to lead a weekend retreat. Five days earlier, I woke up from a "let's just make sure everything is okay" colonoscopy and learned that I had cancer. Two months after my cancer diagnosis, our church was flooded when torrential rain poured over mid-Tennessee. Our worship center and children's wings sustained over $275,000 worth of damage. And a month after the flood, my daughter moved out of our home. She took her sister out to dinner so that her boyfriend and his friends could move her furniture and belongings while she was gone. We'd left both our girls home that weekend, certain they were getting on the bus to youth camp Sunday morning. Instead of getting on that bus, Mikel moved in with her boyfriend and walked away from thousands of dollars of scholarships at a great Christian university. Two weeks later we discovered she was pregnant. About three months after that, my son was diagnosed with mono. He missed three weeks of school and still struggled with a compromised immune system a year later. A month after TJ's mono, my husband had plastic surgery for cancer on his eyelid, and about three weeks after Tom's surgery, my other daughter was diagnosed with the possible beginning of polycystic ovarian syndrome—the same diagnosis I suffered when I dealt with infertility twenty years ago. For years we'd been a healthy and happy family, but the year I wrote *Spiritual Warfare for Women,* we were fraught with disease and syndromes, catastrophic weather, and devastating heartache.

During those days I recognized that in spiritual warfare, there were two battlefronts—no, make that three. The first was with Satan. That didn't surprise me, for I was writing a book about that very thing. The other was with the people and circumstances that Satan messed with. That didn't surprise me either. But the third front surprised me. It was the powerful struggle I had with God. I was surprised by the intensity of that battle. My faith was stripped bare and I came face-to-face with a God I didn't understand. In the book you are holding in your hands, I am sharing the things that God taught me about himself through that part of the war.

How Do I Hear God's Voice?

When my daughter Kaleigh was six, she came into my husband and my bedroom and challenged us with this question: "How do I hear God's voice? I mean, I pray and I hear me talk to Him, but how do I know when He is talking to me?" I tried to give her the good answer I'd been given: "Most of what God has to say He's already written in His Word." I showed her the Bible and told her about Samuel and how he learned to listen to the voice of God. She wasn't satisfied with my answer; she even mentioned that Samuel actually heard God speak with his own ears. I tried to explain that as she grew and read the Bible, she would learn to understand the way God spoke. Sometime later, when she was maybe eight, she came running into the kitchen and exclaimed, "Mama, I get it! I know how God speaks through the Bible! I was reading in Genesis how Cain and Abel didn't get along with one another, and now I know that God is telling me that that is like Mikel and me: We don't get along but I have to be nice." When Kaleigh was eight she began making the connection—the connection between God's Word (the Bible) and her circumstance (getting along with her sister). This is the kind of connection I learned to make as the circumstances in my life grew much worse than sibling rivalry. When we recognize the link between God's Word and our circumstances, we grow in our ability to understand His voice.

When Kaleigh was twelve she came into my bedroom, burdened by things that I wish twelve-year-olds didn't have to be burdened about. One of her friends had recently lost a cousin in a car accident. Another friend was cutting herself, and still another was dealing with her parents' divorce. Kaleigh had promised the friend who was cutting that she would keep her problem a secret, but the secret was causing Kaleigh grief. With tears streaming down her cheeks, she looked at me and said, "Sometimes life just stinks." Kaleigh was right. Sometimes life just stinks. And while this book acknowledges that fact, I want to explore how God uses even the stinky parts of life to reveal himself to us.

Take Hold of God and Don't Let Go

I've met countless women who've let life's troubles consume their faith. Rather than take hold of God and refuse to let Him go, they walk away from God disillusioned and disappointed. Jacob is someone who grabbed hold of God and wouldn't let go. When he wrestled with God, he showed us how to secure God's blessing in the midst of confusing situations. Following his example, you can begin to live in assurance that the God who began a good work in you will be faithful to complete it (Philippians 1:6).

A Woman's Guide to Hearing God's Voice is divided into four parts. In part 1, "Wrestling With God," you will journey with Jacob and his grandfather Abraham. You already know that when disappointment arrives, it brings with it a boatload of unanswered questions that breed doubt. But do you know that those same disappointments can lead you to a wrestling match with God? And do you realize that out of that wrestling match with God you will experience tremendous blessing? Jacob wrestled when the promises of God didn't line up with the picture he'd created in his mind and the reality he was facing. In this part of the book you will learn how to allow your pictures to line up with God's promises and lead you to trust His Person.

In part 2, you will discover the answer to "Where Was God When . . . ?" Where was God when Joseph was in the pit? Where was God when Hezekiah was doing right? Where was God when the disciples were in a storm? By taking a fresh look at some great stories, you will learn to recognize God's presence in your life—whether you're in a pit, doing right, or drenched by waves.

In part 3, "Let God Define Good," you will read the true stories of women I know who have grown through disappointments, crises, and tragedies. Part of learning to hear and respond to the voice of God is coming to places in life where God presses you beyond preconceived notions and limited faith. In this section of the book you will learn how God uses your own "crazy" to teach you new things about yourself and to reveal to you much more of His power and His love.

The final part, "God Will Make a Way," will encourage you to live in expectation of the new thing God is doing in your life. When you live as an intimate companion to Christ, you are His witness to a watching world. As this book draws to a close, I will give you practical steps for writing your own story—a story that features the powerful presence of God and your experience of His perfect love. I will also give you ideas of ways that you might share your story with others.

This book is about being honest with yourself and with God. It's about whipping the Enemy of your faith by allowing God to take the very things that Satan meant for your harm and giving them to God so that He can use *those* things to draw you nearer to Him and to grow you up in your understanding of Him. This book is about embracing the opportunity God gave you to pull back the curtain on the stage of your life and let God reveal himself to those watching you, because they desperately long to see God as He truly is, perfect in love and powerful in presence.

Are you eager to hear the voice of God? Are the struggles in your life drowning out His voice? Do you want God to bless you? Are you willing to hold on tight? If so, this book is for you.

Being confident of this, that he who began a good work in you will carry it on to completion until the day of Christ Jesus.

Philippians 1:6

PART ONE

Wrestling With God

I have a dear friend, Mrs. Anna. She lives in a restored farmhouse that is graced by a wraparound porch. When she entertains, everyone who sits at her dining room table eats with silver, drinks sweet tea from crystal goblets, and seasons their farm-fresh meal from little dishes that hold individual servings of salt and pepper. Mrs. Anna raises free-range chickens, grows vegetables that she gathers in baskets, and has some of the most beautiful Knock Out roses you can imagine. She's lived long enough to be wise, and one day she shared her wisdom with me.

"Leighann, there are times in our lives when we find ourselves wrestling with our angels." She told me that her mother used to explain to her that when things were not going her way—when life wasn't making sense—it was an invitation to take hold of God's promises, wrestle with them, and never let go, just like Jacob. I love the visual image of taking hold of God, hanging on tight, and insisting that He bless me.

> Wrestling with God is not a bad thing. It's impossible to wrestle with someone who is far away from you. You can only wrestle someone who is close to you. Sometimes we interpret it as failure, but I think God sees it as intimacy.
>
> —A counselor named Chuck[1]

1. Jon Acuff, "What's your favorite quote?" entry from Ana "Jacob" Sofia, Stuff Christians Like, accessed March 1, 2013, www.jonacuff.com/stuffchristians like/2011/01/whats-your-favorite-quote/.

1

Hearing God's Voice 101

> Moses approached the thick darkness where God was.
>
> Exodus 20:21

I wish it were as easy to write this book as it is to teach a class. I wish that I could give you a syllabus, prepare lectures, and let you complete a test so that you could drink it in—*it* being the ability to hear God's voice. But *it's* not that easy. Sometimes God invites us, like He invited Moses, into the "thick darkness" and communicates with us there. That's what this book is about—going into the darkness and meeting God there. But before we head to those dark places, let's lay down some general rules about how God communicates with us.

God Usually Does Not Communicate With Us Audibly

First, God most often does not communicate with us audibly. I know, it seems a bit odd that He would give us ears—two, in fact—and expect us to use them to listen to one another when we communicate and then choose not to put those ears to use when He communicates with us. I don't know why He does this, but He does. I've never yet heard the voice of God with my ears . . . not yet. I am open to that, but God hasn't chosen to speak to me in that way.

God Communicates With Us Through His Word

Second, God most often communicates with us through His Word, the Bible. And while the Bible itself is an ancient collection of sixty-six books, it is the inspired revelation of God as recorded through the ages. You have perhaps heard the Bible referred to as the inerrant Word of God. When people say that, they mean that they believe the Bible has been set apart by God to be the complete and perfect disclosure of himself to us. In between "In the beginning, God . . ." in Genesis 1:1 and "Amen" in Revelation 22:21, God lets us know who He is, how He interacts with mankind, and more than anything else how much He loves us. I've heard some refer to the Bible as God's collection of love letters to us.

In order to experience the difference between reading the Bible for information and reading it for inspiration, you need to have a personal relationship with God. When you enter in to a personal relationship with God (by repenting of your sins, accepting Jesus as your Savior, and determining to live your life under God's direction), you receive a marvelous gift, the gift of the Holy Spirit. The Holy Spirit *in* you reveals truth. He takes Scripture and brings it to life. Where once you might have read a chapter or a verse and thought, *That's interesting,* the Holy Spirit will take that chapter or verse and open your mind and heart to understand how it relates to you *right where you are.* Then you will read it and think, *That's for me!*

You Must Read the Bible in Order to Hear God Speak

Because God most often communicates through His Word, you need to read it. It doesn't matter how living and active God's Word might be; if you don't take time to read the Bible, you won't benefit from the power of it. When you read the Bible, it is good to read for information, to learn more about God—but also to read for inspiration, to experience more of God.

What is the difference? When you read for information, you might read the Bible much like you would a history book, taking note of dates and names, places and time periods. It is good to understand the cultures that set the context for the biblical writers. As you read for information, you grow in your understanding of God's character and His ways. This helps you to discern His voice when He speaks to you.

When you read the Bible for inspiration, you approach a particular passage of Scripture with this prayer on your lips: "Lord, I need to hear a word from you today. Please, speak to me through your Word; help me to hear and to understand what you are saying to me." When you make a habit of reading God's Word on a daily basis, and you pray that prayer, you will experience the power of God's Word. The words you read will jump off the pages of the book into your heart and mind. Then you will say, "God spoke this to me in His Word today. . . ."

Obey God's Word If You Want to Hear His Voice

You must be willing to obey God's instructions (as presented in His Word) in order to hear His voice. God tells you what to do, and then He waits patiently for your obedience before He says anything else. Many people suffer the silence of God because they refuse to respond to the prompting of His Spirit. There is a whole lot of mystery surrounding the activity of the Holy Spirit.

Don't get confused by Him. God is Father, Son, and Holy Spirit. Each aspect of His Person reaches into our lives to draw us into a personal relationship with Him. God the Father sent His Son to provide us with this relationship. The Holy Spirit comes to abide (or live) in us when we enter into a relationship with God. It is the Holy Spirit who speaks to us when we read God's Word. The Holy Spirit guides us into truth.

Many years ago my daughter Mikel asked Jesus into her heart and followed her decision with baptism. She was six years old. At the time I wondered if she truly understood what she was doing, but I didn't stand in the way because I kept hearing the voice of Jesus when He told His disciples, "Let the little children come to me, and do not hinder them, for the kingdom of God belongs to such as these" (Mark 10:14). When Mikel was in sixth grade she confided in me that she thought God wanted her to be baptized again because she didn't fully understand what she was doing when she was six. I encouraged her to be baptized, but she was too afraid of what others would think, so she didn't do it. She made me promise not to tell her father, and I chose not to press the issue. I trusted that what she was dealing with was between her and God, not her and me and God.

A few years passed and Mikel was fifteen. She was having a difficult time juggling her friendships, softball, and school. One afternoon she cried as she shared her frustration, stress, and confusion with me. I encouraged her to pray and talk with God about these things. She responded to my urging with this: "Mom, I've tried to do that, but God doesn't talk to me like He talks to you. It just doesn't work for me."

Her words broke my heart, and I knew they were not true. God doesn't choose to be real to one person and not to another. Something was amiss. So I asked Mikel, "When was the last time you know you heard God's voice?" She looked at me with tears streaming down her cheeks and said, "You know." I didn't know, I'd forgotten. But then I remembered—I remembered the day she'd told me that she thought she needed to be baptized because she understood better what it meant to accept Jesus as Savior and Lord. I also knew that Mikel had chosen to ignore that prompting of the Spirit of God for several years. So this is what I said: "Mikel, many times God tells us something that He wants us to do. Then He waits. He waits to see if we will obey Him. And if we do, He tells us something else. When we choose to obey His voice, we know He's there and He walks with us through the confusing stuff life throws our way. But if we don't obey Him, He remains silent. We're kind of on our own until we choose to obey Him."

Mikel understood. Two weeks later, at fifteen years old, she was baptized by her weeping father. Mikel wanted to hear God's voice, so she chose to obey His Word. She obeyed in spite of her fear, in spite of her embarrassment, and in spite of what other people might think. In fact, she invited her friends and her softball team to come and witness her baptism. We celebrated with family, friends, and teammates at a barbecue after church. I don't think I've ever been prouder of her than when she stood in the baptismal waters that day.

God Communicates With Us Through Other People

God communicates with us through other believers. When Jesus came to walk on earth, He chose twelve men to be His disciples. Those men walked and talked and lived with Jesus for three years. Through that experience, eleven of them started a movement that continues to impact the world today. Through those men Jesus built the church. Right after Jesus ascended into heaven, His followers stood there staring into the sky. Two angels appeared to those disciples and questioned the value of their star gazing, so they returned to Jerusalem. When they got back to Jerusalem, they gathered together in a room to pray. Can you imagine what it might have been like to be in that room? Acts 1:15 tells us that there were about 120 men and women present at the prayer meeting.

I don't know how long the disciples prayed, but Peter stood up among them and spoke to them. He led the people to choose a replacement for Judas the traitor (Matthias was the one they chose). God spoke to His disciples through Peter. Ever since that day God has chosen men and women to speak His Word. Our pastors do this every Sunday when they stand in their pulpits and discuss God's Word. We do this with one another when we share a verse or a word of encouragement with a friend.

I've often been impressed with God's method of repeating himself when He speaks through others. I will read something in my quiet time and know that it is a "word" for me. How will I know? Allow me to explain. Let's say my heart is heavy because my daughter is unhappy at college. I'll be reading the Psalms and come across Psalm 37:3–4:

> Trust in the Lord and do good; dwell in the land and enjoy safe pasture. Take delight in the Lord, and he will give you the desires of your heart.

I will smile when I read that because my daughter is walking with God. She reads her Bible, prays, and seeks godly companions to encourage her along the way. I know that she's trusting God, and I know that she's "doing good," and therefore I am confident that God will give her the desires of her heart. I pray for her and, if I'm really a good mom, I'll jot her a note and put it in the mail. Later that same day I might be listening to the radio when a recording artist will share how God used Psalm 37:4 in his life during a difficult season. I'll smile to myself as I drive north on Highway 31 and know that God is speaking to me. Then, at lunch I'll be talking to a friend about what's going on in her life, and she might mention Psalm 37:4 again. Has that ever happened to you? When it does, you will know that you are hearing God's voice!

God Communicates Through Praise and Worship

The sixth general rule is that God speaks through praise and worship. I've seen men and women sit in our worship services at Thompson Station Church and literally cry through the entire service because their hearts are so hungry for a word from God. Their tears are tears of release and relief. At our church we worship God. Our choir and band don't perform, they lead in worship. And as we lift our voices (and sometimes our hands), the presence of God fills the worship center. Scripture says that God inhabits the praises of His people (Psalm 22:3 KJV).

There was one Sunday when our pastor (who is my husband) stood silently while the choir hummed behind him. He was being still and listening rather than speaking. In the silence, different people across the congregation spontaneously began to share Scripture aloud. Their voices could be heard first to the left, then to the right, and somewhere in the back center of the room. Our education pastor's son pulled on his daddy's arm and whispered in his ear, "Is that God speaking?" Pastor Louis told his son that in a way it was! God's people were speaking God's Word aloud in the room, and through that experience of worship we were hearing the voice of God.

God Sometimes Communicates With Us Through Visions

The Bible records several stories of God communicating with individuals through visions. Sometimes those visions came in the form of dreams (as in Joseph and Pharaoh's case), and sometimes they seemed to be actual experiences (as in the case of some of the prophets). In Joel 2:28 we are told that young men will see visions and old men will dream dreams. Although this is not a common way that God chooses to communicate with me, He has given me both visions and dreams on very rare occasions. I share a few of these experiences in my book *Oh God, Please Help Me With My Doubt* (Worthy Publishers). You will read about one of my visions later in this book.

Be sure to realize that when God speaks to you through visions and/or dreams, His message will always line up with His Word.

You Will Not Hear God's Voice Unless You Cultivate an Attitude of Gratitude

The eighth general rule, and this will be the final one, is this: You will not hear the voice of God apart from cultivating an attitude of gratitude in your life. If you go through life always looking at your glass half empty, you will miss the ability to hear God speak. Paul warned the believers in Rome of this hindrance to hearing the voice of God.

> For although they knew God, they neither glorified him as God nor gave thanks to him, but their thinking became futile and their foolish hearts were darkened.
>
> Romans 1:21

When you get to a place in your life where you fail to acknowledge God's goodness toward you—when you get too busy, or too burdened, or too full of pride to thank Him for His faithfulness and His love—you will find it hard to hear His voice. Later in Romans 1, Paul went on to say that those same people who "neither glorified God nor gave thanks to him" were given over by God to the sinful desires of their hearts. "They exchanged the truth about God for a lie, and worshiped and served created things rather than the Creator" (Romans 1:25). Eventually they participated in unnatural desires (specifically homosexuality). They were eaten up with envy, greed, and depravity. Their culture was filled with murder, strife, deceit, and malice. They were slanderers, gossips, and God-haters who were insolent, arrogant, and boastful. They invented ways of doing evil; they disobeyed their parents; they were senseless, faithless, heartless, and ruthless. (See Romans 1:21–32.) And it all began with a failure to glorify (worship) God and give Him thanks. You will not hear God's voice without cultivating an attitude of gratitude in your life.

Approaching God in the Darkness

Those are the general rules regarding hearing God's voice. If I were preparing a class on hearing the voice of God, those eight things would be what I would teach:

1. God usually does not communicate with us audibly.
2. God communicates with us through His Word (the Bible).
3. You have to read the Bible to hear God speak.
4. You must be willing to obey His instructions to hear Him speak.
5. God communicates with us through other believers.
6. God speaks through praise and worship.
7. God sometimes speaks through dreams and visions.
8. You must cultivate an attitude of gratitude in your life in order to hear God's voice.

In the rest of this book I want to show you how God communicates with us in the darkness. The verse I chose to open this chapter was Exodus 20:21, "Moses approached the thick darkness where God was."

Sometimes the circumstances of life create a thick darkness. Because we tend to be afraid of what we cannot see, our natural response to darkness is to flee. But because God was *in* the darkness, and Moses wanted to hear His voice, he boldly approached the darkness. My hope is that as you read this book, you will become like Moses and eagerly approach the thick darkness, knowing that God is there.

A few years ago I felt like the darkness surrounding me was swallowing me alive. I took my heavy heart (and my husband) to our prayer clinic. The prayer clinic at Thompson Station Church is a place where people come for prayer—much like a medical clinic is a place people go when they are sick. Our prayer clinic is staffed with men and women who have the gift of intercession. The entire army of intercessors surrounded us in prayer.

During that prayer time, my sweet friend Julie began to pray an interesting prayer. It went something like this: "Oh, gracious Father, we know that you love our pastor and his wife. We know that nothing can come against them that hasn't first been brought before your throne. And although this situation they are in today is breaking their hearts, we believe that you have allowed it because you want to take them with you into the deep, dark, and secret places where your most valuable treasures are hidden. As you lead them in the dark, Lord, make them aware of your presence. And don't let their own suffering stop them from collecting every single treasure you have for them there."

Hers was a prayer that went deeper than my comfort and joy. Part of me wanted to scream, "No, God! I don't want those things no matter how precious they might be." You see, I don't like bats, and I don't like spiders, and I don't like those creepy-crawly things that slink along on a bazillion little legs. I don't like to slosh in muddy water where I can't see my toes and it's cold and damp and dark. I'd just as soon not go there. But the part of me that surrendered all that I was to all that I understood God to be when I was eleven years old at a girls' camp in the north Georgia mountains knew that if God was taking me into the deep, dark places where He kept His most valuable treasures, then I was going every step of the way with Him.

I've been spiritually spelunking for a couple years now. And I've collected a few treasures along the way. It's those gems I've uncovered that I want to polish with you now. From this point forward I want you to embrace these eight "givens" about hearing God's voice, and then come with me as we approach the thick darkness where God is.

Treasure Hunt

This is a great book to study with a small group of friends. Simply read the chapters on your own, then reflect on the questions listed at the end of each chapter. When you get together, answer the discussion questions, share insights from God's Word, and pray together. Consider memorizing the "treasure verse" and collecting the precious jewels. A fun activity might be to make a bracelet or a necklace to commemorate the journey that you take with one another.

Personal Reflection

- Review the eight general rules. Which way does God most often speak to you?
- What part of the "thick darkness" scares you? Consider admitting your fear and asking God to give you courage to go wherever He wants you to go as you walk with Him.

Discussion Questions

1. Share a time when you "heard" the voice of God while reading the Bible.
2. Share a time when your obedience (or lack of) affected your ability to hear the voice of God.
3. Are you facing the "thick darkness"? If you are, share the darkness you are facing and invite your friends to pray for you as you move ahead in your treasure hunt.

4. Take turns offering quick prayers of thanksgiving for the many ways that God has blessed you this week. (By doing this you are cultivating an attitude of gratitude.)

Treasure Verse

Moses approached the thick darkness where God was.

Exodus 20:21

2

Jacob's Story

Oh Lord, please rescue me from the hand of my brother, Esau. I
am afraid that he is coming to attack me, along with my wives and
children. But you promised me, "I will surely treat you kindly, and
I will multiply your descendants until they become as numerous as
the sands along the seashore—too many to count."

Genesis 32:11–12 NLT

The best part of walking in the darkness with God is the proximity of His presence. Unlike walking in the light, the darkness
demands that you feel your way forward by walking right next to
your Guide; so close that your skin touches His and you sense the
warmth of His presence guiding you every step of the way. Sometimes, in the midst of that darkness, if you are really confident in
God's goodness and really confused by His ways, you just might
take hold of Him and refuse to let go, just like Jacob did.

In this chapter you will discover that God uses people who
struggle to tell the truth, who manipulate others, and who have a
hard time getting along with family members and friends. You will
also learn that following God might plant you right at the "ford of
the Jabbok," where obedience to Him seems to spell disaster for

your own life, for the lives of those you love, and for the dreams that you thought God gave you. Then in the next chapter you will discover that when you come to that place, you too can take hold of God and wrestle with Him until He accomplishes His purposes in your life.

Wrestling With Your Angel

I mentioned my dear friend Mrs. Anna earlier. Besides her charm in Southern hospitality, I most enjoy her tried-and-true wisdom. I'll never forget the day she shared with me that sometimes we find ourselves "wrestling with our angels." Her mother shared this wisdom with her as she encouraged her daughter to take hold of ALL God's promises and refuse to let them go.

As Mrs. Anna described angel wrestling with me, I couldn't help but think of Jacob. Jacob was a wrestler. Scripture tells us that even when he was in his mother's womb he wrestled with his twin brother, Esau. The book of Genesis takes us on a journey through Jacob's life, where we discover that he never stopped wrestling—ever! Jacob was the kind of guy who took hold of what he wanted and manipulated and connived others into giving him what they had, sometimes even against their wishes. But he didn't always win; many times Jacob was manipulated as well. He received what he dished out. But the part of Jacob's story that I like most is the part that happened at the ford of the Jabbok, the night Jacob wrestled with God and won. I like this part best because I'm a woman who wants to press in close to God and wrestle Him for His blessing. I would imagine that you are too, that's why you're reading this book. Any woman interested in hearing the voice of God is most definitely interested in experiencing His blessing on her life. But before we get to Jacob's wrestling match, let's take a look at the experiences that led him there.

Jacob's Life

A walk through Genesis 25–31 will give us a quick view of Jacob's wrestling skills.

Genesis 25: Jacob grasped Esau's heel during birth. And although Esau won that wrestling match and was born first, Jacob never really let go of his heel (figuratively speaking). After Jacob and Esau grew up, Jacob enticed Esau to trade his birthright for a bowl of stew. In a terrible trade spurred by Esau's willingness to exchange long-term gain for immediate gratification, Esau traded away the double portion of his father's land and the authority that was rightfully his for the instant satisfaction of a stew Jacob prepared.

Genesis 27: After making that inequitable trade (Esau's birthright for Jacob's stew), Jacob tricked Esau and stole his father's blessing from him. Isaac's blessing (intended for Esau) was a transference of God's favor on his son. Isaac intended to name Esau as the next in line to receive the special covenant relationship with God that had begun with Abraham and been passed down to Isaac. Jacob deceived his father by pretending to be Esau, then he secured Esau's blessing for himself. I can only imagine the tempers that raged in Isaac's home that day. I would daresay that if their neighbors lived as close to them as some of ours do to us, they could have heard the shouting. Esau was most likely bitter over the trade he'd made, but in trading away his birthright he knew that he had only himself to blame. When Jacob deceptively stole Esau's blessing, Esau became so angry that he plotted to kill his brother (Genesis 27:41). So Jacob ran for his life.

Genesis 29: But what goes around comes around, and when Jacob got to Haran, his uncle Laban deceived him. After working seven years for Rachel's hand in marriage, Jacob was tricked into marrying Rachel's sister, Leah, instead. Jacob's uncle made him work seven more years for Rachel. Did you wear a veil when you were married? Did your groom lift the veil to kiss his bride? The tradition of the wedding veil dates back to arranged marriages. The bride would be veiled so that the groom could not judge her based on her appearance and thus refuse to marry her. However, the Jewish culture has traditionally allowed men to choose their own wives. In the Jewish wedding ceremony, the groom actually places the veil on his bride so that he knows who it is that is hiding under there. This tradition began because of what Laban did to Jacob (so tradition says).

Genesis 30: Jacob struck a deal with Laban and then used his understanding of sheep and goat husbandry to grow extremely prosperous with his flocks.

Genesis 31: Even after Jacob had lived and worked with his uncle Laban and Laban's sons (Jacob's cousins) for many years, the family ties were not strong enough to hold back rising tensions. Laban and his sons were greedy, and when they saw Jacob's prosperity they resented him. Their attitude toward Jacob changed. So Jacob left his uncle Laban and decided it was time to return to his own land . . . the land God promised to give him just after he'd fled from Esau many years before.

Chosen by God

Although Jacob might be considered a scoundrel today, God chose him to be the next in line for the blessing He promised his grandfather, Abraham. God's promise to Jacob is found in Genesis 28:10–22. Go get your Bible and read it for yourself. But don't read it nonchalantly. Take time to put yourself just on the other side of the stone that Jacob used as a pillow. In Genesis 28, Jacob has already cheated his brother out of his birthright and deceived his father. He was running for his life, leaving all that he'd known behind. Read God's promise carefully and imagine what it might have been like to be Jacob hearing it for the first time.

When Jacob rested his head on that rock, he was not only running for his life but also grieving the loss of his mother and his father (whom he would never see again this side of heaven). Perhaps he'd even had time to think about all that had happened, and those tormenting thoughts made his journey all the lonelier. Guilt, regret, shame had all set in, and on top of that he had blisters on his feet and only a rock for a pillow.

But exhaustion took over and Jacob slept. His worn-out sleep led to a dream. In his dream Jacob heard God's voice. At a time when he might have anticipated righteous indignation and condemnation from the God of the father he'd just deceived, Jacob instead received some powerful promises. Right after God assured Jacob that he was still a part of the special family God chose to share a covenant relationship with Him, He went on to promise the following:

1. I will give you and your descendants THIS land. (Genesis 28:13)
2. I will give you many descendants. (Genesis 28:14)
3. Everyone on earth will be blessed through you and your offspring. (Genesis 28:14)
4. I will be with you. I will watch over you wherever you go. (Genesis 28:15)
5. I will bring you back here. (Genesis 28:15)
6. I will not leave you until I have done what I have promised you. (Genesis 28:15)

Think about that for a minute. Jacob was greedy, he was crafty, and he manipulated people. Jacob always put himself in the forefront of his thoughts and actions. You know anybody like that? Does that seem like the kind of person God would choose to use? Maybe not, but God chose Jacob.

The morning after Jacob's unusual night, he declared the place where God met him in his dream to be awesome (Genesis 28:17).

He took the stone that served as a pillow for his head and set it up as an altar. He worshiped there by pouring oil over that stone and called that place Bethel, which means "house of God." Jacob believed that somehow his frantic escape from Esau led him straight to God's house. Then he made a tremendous promise in response to that God moment in his life. Jacob promised to faithfully tithe a tenth of his income to God if God would watch over him, provide for him, and one day return him safely to his father's house. I can almost sense the humility and reverence that Jacob had as he knelt by that stone.

Don't you imagine that dream planted a picture in Jacob's head? Don't you imagine that from that moment forward, Jacob forever remembered that rock? Don't you imagine that Jacob, during those long years of laboring for Laban, might have laid his head on a stone in Laban's pastures and dreamed of the day when he would experience the fulfillment of God's promises?

I do!

Living in Expectation of God

When we wrestle with God, we find ourselves there because we have lived for years in expectation of what God promised us He would do. Just like Jacob, we anchor our hope on something we read or an experience we had with God. Many of us deposited our hopes and dreams in the bank of God's love and sealed them with Jeremiah 29:11: "'For I know the plans I have for you,' declares the Lord, 'plans to prosper you and not to harm you, plans to give you hope and a future.'"

I've no doubt that Jacob's dream at Bethel lingered with him through all the miserable years he spent with Laban in Paddan Aram. It was the dream that God planted in Jacob's heart, a dream full of promise that caused Jacob to wake up one morning, after twenty years of service in Laban's house, and notice that Uncle Laban and his sons weren't smiling. They had a look in their eyes that was not friendly. Something was noticeably different about them, and Jacob sensed that he wasn't their favorite nephew/cousin. After years of working for his uncle Laban, Jacob knew it was time to leave him and return to his home. He was no doubt homesick (he'd tried to leave earlier, but Laban wouldn't let him go). So Jacob ran away (he'd developed a pattern of running from difficult circumstances earlier in his life). Off he went, but Laban ran after him.

When Laban caught up with him, Jacob went into a tirade and described how difficult the past twenty years had been. Turn to Genesis 31:38–42 and read it for yourself. Jacob told Laban that he cheated him, mistreated him, and made life difficult for him. He wouldn't have made it had it not been for his heritage and God's intervention. Laban whined a bit and felt sorry for himself. Finally that bitter encounter ended with Jacob and Laban making a covenant with one another. They swore to part "friends" and promised never to return again to each other. It's sort of sad—the part where Laban kissed his daughters and grandchildren good-bye and then returned home.

But the story continues right on into Genesis 32. Just after the unpleasant confrontation with his uncle, Jacob faced the potential wrath of his estranged brother, Esau. As much as Jacob might have dreaded that confrontation with Laban, it was nothing compared to the fear he most likely experienced as he traveled closer to the inevitable encounter he was about to have with his twin brother. For unlike the relationship Jacob had with Laban, he was not a victim in relationship to Esau. Jacob was the perpetrator.

I have to stop here and wonder, *What possessed Jacob to go back to Esau?* Of all the places Jacob could have gone, why go back toward home? It had to be the message Jacob heard from God when He met him in his dream in Genesis 28. When Jacob laid his head on that rock, God painted a picture of his future. That picture included possession of the land where Jacob lay when he had his dream. When God paints a picture in our hearts and minds, we are never completely satisfied until the picture we carry within us is released to be reality outside of us.

I would imagine that you can trace your own story back to a time in your life when you trusted God to fulfill your hopes and dreams. In your innocence you believed Him. But now you move forward, perhaps even with fear and trembling. Today you are willing to confront the skeletons of your past because God has directed your life thus far and you are almost certain that He has your treasure just on the other side of that person (or situation) that stands between you and your promise.

While God promised Jacob possession of the land, prosperity, and lots of descendants, we find him in Genesis 32 standing by the ford of the Jabbok surrounded by everything God had given him—all that is precious to him. We smile at the scene, but just as we're about to pull out the hot dogs for a weenie roast, Jacob's messengers return to report that his brother, Esau, is on his way, and four hundred men are coming with him.

Perhaps you are in the same place today. You have this picture in your mind, one that God painted when you were young. Perhaps, way back then, you too made mistakes. Maybe those mistakes include broken relationships with your family. A long time ago you might have been frightened and found yourself running away from all that was familiar to you.

Perhaps you weren't. Maybe you were like me, sitting on the edge of a desert and watching the sunset, yielding your life to God, and trusting Him to fill it with whatever He saw fit to put in and out of your life. You trusted Him because all that you'd known thus far was His goodness and His grace.

Whether you were running afraid, or walking in faith, God gave you a picture of your life. His picture was filled with promise and purpose and good stuff. But today, even surrounded by the "so much" that God has done in your life, you face a situation that threatens to destroy it all. What will you do?

Jacob prayed.

Treasures Hidden in the Dark

This prayer that Jacob prayed serves as a great model for us when we find ourselves postured for a wrestling match with God. Notice, though, that Jacob didn't kneel in full confidence clothed in courage. His isn't a prayer of "great faith" anchored in the certainty of things not seen. Jacob's prayer is an honest crying out for God to come through for him. Look at Genesis 32:9–12.

> Then Jacob prayed, "O God of my father Abraham, God of my father Isaac, Lord, you who said to me, 'Go back to your country and your relatives, and I will make you prosper,' I am unworthy of all the kindness and faithfulness you have shown your servant. I had only my staff when I crossed this Jordan, but now I have become two camps. Save me, I pray, from the hand of my brother Esau, for I am afraid he will come and attack me, and also the mothers with their children. But you have said, 'I will surely make you prosper and will make your descendants like the sand of the sea, which cannot be counted.'"

I love this prayer! It's honest, it's direct, and it's filled with God's very own words. Do you need to pray a prayer like this one? Take a closer look:

1. Jacob remembered who God is. "O God of my father Abraham, God of my father Isaac, Lord, you who said to me . . ." (v. 9).
2. Jacob reminded God of what He told him to do, and what He promised would happen when he obeyed. *"Go back to your country and your relatives, and I will make you prosper. . . . I will surely make you prosper and will make your descendants like the sand of the sea, which cannot be counted"* (vv. 9 and 12).
3. Jacob acknowledged what God had already done for him. *"I am unworthy of all the kindness and faithfulness you have shown your servant. I had only my staff when I crossed this Jordan, but now I have become two camps"* (v. 10).

4. Jacob confessed his fear. (This is the honest part that I like.) *"Save me, I pray, from the hand of my brother Esau, for I am afraid he will come and attack me, and also the mothers with their children"* (v. 11).

5. Jacob professed his faith (anchored in God's promise). *"But you have said, 'I will surely make you prosper and will make your descendants like the sand of the sea, which cannot be counted'"* (v. 12).

This is a great prayer to use as a model for your own. If you feel like you are standing next to the ford of the Jabbok, pressed forward by faith and back by fear, pray like Jacob prayed.

1. Remember who God is.
2. Remind God of what He told you to do, and what He promised He would do for you when you obeyed Him.
3. Acknowledge all of the things that God has already done for you.
4. Confess your fear (go ahead, God knows it is there).
5. Profess your faith, and anchor your profession of faith in the promise of God.

When you use Jacob's model prayer as your own, you will experience God's direction and peace in the midst of your mess.

Treasure Hunt

Personal Reflections

- Read Jacob's story in Genesis 27–33 and 35.
- Think back to the early days of your walk with the Lord. What were your concerns?
- What were your dreams?

- How has God fulfilled them?
- Have you ever been (or are you now) at the ford of the Jabbok? Describe what your situation looks like. How is it similar to Jacob's? How is it different?

Discussion Questions

1. How has God blessed your life?
2. What triggers a crisis of belief in your life?
3. As a group, pray like Jacob prayed.
   a. Take turns remembering who God is.
   b. Share some of the promises that He's given you.
   c. Each one of you list at least five things God has done for you.
   d. If you are at a place in your life where you are afraid or uncertain—confess your fear.
   e. Profess your faith, and anchor it in a promise from God's Word. (Check appendix 1 for promises to claim.)

Treasure Verse

The Lord is trustworthy in all he promises and faithful in all he does.

Psalm 145:13

3

Wrestling With God

When the man saw that he could not overpower him, he touched the socket of Jacob's hip so that his hip was wrenched as he wrestled with the man. The man said, "Let me go, for it is daybreak." But Jacob replied, "I will not let you go unless you bless me."

Genesis 32:25–26

At the end of the previous chapter we took a very close look at Jacob's prayer. It is a good prayer. I mentioned that I especially like it because it is direct, honest, and filled with God's own words. It is always good to pray back to God what He has promised to you. God loves for us to hold Him to His promises. But sometimes when I pray, even when I pray good prayers, I finish my prayer and feel just as afraid, confused, and uncertain as I did before I prayed. God doesn't always come down in my prayer time and remove my fear. He doesn't often send me a message on heavenly parchment to let me know that He'll see me through. Unlike Elisha's servant, whose eyes were opened to see God's chariots camped on the hillside (2 Kings 6), my eyes remain shut after I utter "Amen." I open my eyes after I pray and don't see anything but trouble. I love the continued story of Jacob, because he finished his great prayer and felt just like I often do when I finish mine.

Wrestling With God

Jacob prayed, and when he was done, he did all he could do to prepare for the inevitable encounter with his brother. He sent gifts (in hopes of appeasing Esau's anger), and he organized his family (for the best defense he could possibly create). Jacob did his part; he prayed and he prepared, but still he feared the worst. After all was said and done, Jacob's fear was still real and he wasn't any closer to a guaranteed victory, so . . . he wrestled with God.

> So Jacob was left alone, and a man wrestled with him till daybreak. When the man saw that he could not overpower him, he touched the socket of Jacob's hip so that his hip was wrenched as he wrestled with the man. The man said, "Let me go, for it is daybreak." But Jacob replied, "I will not let you go unless you bless me."
>
> Genesis 32:24–26

Did Jacob wrestle with a man, an angel, or God?

In Genesis 32:24–32 Jacob wrestled with God. Whether God manifested himself in the form of a man or sent an angel to represent himself, the heart of the struggle was personal. It was a wrestling match between Jacob and God.

Some scholars believe that Jacob wrestled with God in bodily form. Others believe that he wrestled with an angel who represented God. The Scripture calls Jacob's opponent "a man," but an ordinary man cannot "wrench" a hip out of socket with a simple touch (v. 25). In order for Jacob to enter into a wrestling match that lasted all night, he had to be wrestling with a body similar to his own. Those who believe the body was inhabited by God point to verses 29–30:

"Please tell me your name," Jacob said. "Why do you want to know my name?" the man replied. Then he blessed Jacob there. Jacob named the place Peniel (which means "face of God"), for he said, "I have seen God face to face, yet my life has been spared."

Genesis 32:29–30 NLT

Jacob recognized the miracle of his unusual encounter with God. To "see God face to face" and live was to be granted an intimacy that was rare. Later, Moses begged for the opportunity to see God's face, and his request was denied (Exodus 33:18–20). God told Moses that no one could see His face and live. Jacob apparently knew this truth, and that was why he was humbled by his encounter.

Those who believe that Jacob wrestled with an angel point to the holiness of God. God's holiness sets Him apart from people. Therefore God must have sent an angel representative to participate in this personal encounter with Jacob. If Jacob's opponent was an angel, he did not identify himself as one (which is rare). But if he was an angel, he still came on assignment from God and fully represented God. Hosea 12:4 actually calls Jacob's wrestling partner "an angel," but Hosea uses this interchangeably with "God" (see Hosea 12:3).

I believe God took on human form and wrestled with Jacob. But I'm not going to argue with those who insist He sent an angel to fulfill this assignment. I am more amazed that Jacob was able to go toe-to-toe with a supernatural being. The only explanation is that Jacob's wrestling partner either chose to limit his own strength to equal that of Jacob, or God supernaturally strengthened Jacob so that he could wrestle as an equal to his partner.

Ben Patterson, in the *Prayer Devotional Bible,* says this about Jacob's wrestling match with God:

God loves this kind of wrestling. Not much good comes from wrestling with other people: resentment rises and enemies are made. Not much good comes from wrestling with life and work either: sleep becomes elusive and ulcers form. "In vain you rise early and stay

44

up late, toiling for food to eat" (Psalm 127:2). "Toiling" is another word for fruitless wrestling.

Instead of "toiling," take it to the Lord in prayer. Wrestle with Him for the blessing, [don't wrestle] with people and circumstances.

Resist God in the sense of rejecting God, and you will not be able to resist any evil. But resist God in the sense of closing with God, cling to Him with your strength, not your weakness only . . . and He will give you strength. Cast yourself into His arms not to be caressed but to wrestle with Him. He loves that holy war. He may be too many for you, and lift you from your feet. But it will be to lift you from the earth, and set you in the heavenly places which [are given as a reward to those] who fight the good fight and lay hold of God as their eternal life.[1]

What a wrestling match! I love the part of Ben Patterson's commentary that assures us that God "loves that holy war." Jacob, a mere man, afraid, vulnerable, and completely at the mercy of God, versus the Lord Almighty, the ultimate power of heaven. Is it just me, or do you too find it interesting that, while Jacob was terrified of his brother, he didn't hesitate to take on God? I love that! Somehow in the twenty years of being on the opposite side of a greedy man's selfish ambition (working for his uncle Laban), Jacob grew close enough in his walk with God to enter into a wrestling match.

I did a bit of research about angels for my book *Spiritual Warfare for Women* and discovered that they are both wiser and stronger than people. And since Scripture calls Jacob's opponent an angel (Hosea 12:4), I agree with Ron Dunn's take on Jacob's wrestling match with God:

Do you believe Jacob was so strong he could pin down an angel? *That fight was fixed!* I believe that while the angel was saying, "Let me go," he was whispering under his breath, "But I hope you don't. Hang on a little while longer and you'll get the blessing."[2]

1. Ben Patterson, *Prayer Devotional Bible* (Grand Rapids, MI: Zondervan), 42.
2. Ronald Dunn, *Don't Just Stand There, Pray Something* (Nashville: Thomas Nelson), 78.

My Invitation to Wrestle

We don't often take hold of God like Jacob did unless we have nowhere else to turn and no one else to turn to. A few years ago I was diagnosed with colon cancer. The word *cancer* was almost synonymous with death in my mind. But I've learned that we've come a very long way in the medical field, and just because one has cancer does not mean that she will die. I'm living proof that you can be diagnosed with cancer and still live—quite well. In fact, I was baffled by my short experience with cancer. I was diagnosed on March 1, and after surgery, I was declared cancer free on March 26. But I learned that once you have cancer, you enter a long-term relationship with your very own oncologist, who insists on seeing you every three to six months for the rest of your life.

Just three weeks ago I was sitting in my doctor's office, waiting for her to tell me that my CT scan was good and my blood levels were great, so I could check "Doctor visit" off my list of things to do, and hopefully not have to return for another six months. That was when she said, "Your CEA number has jumped up."

"How much up?" I asked.

"It's just about tripled," she answered.

"What?!" How could that be? I was cancer free! I was healthy! I was coming to these appointments as a formality—they weren't supposed to find anything wrong. And immediately my thoughts went to all the reasons I need to live. *My daughter Mikel and my granddaughter, Misty, need me. My daughter Kaleigh is changing schools—she needs me. My son, TJ, hasn't even graduated high school yet—he needs me. And don't even get me started on Tom . . . what would he possibly do without me?*

So here I am again. They've actually found a "shadow" on my liver and are assuming that it is the return of my cancer. I'm headed to see a surgeon next week. According to my oncologist, it's "no big deal, we'll just cut it out and be done with it." But it seems like a big deal to me.

So I'm wrestling with God. I'm pressing in close where CEA numbers and shadows don't exist unless the sovereign hand of my Lord and Savior decide that they do. I'm holding tight because I want to live a few more years and write a few more books (make that forty more years and at least ten more books).

Cancer is the ford of the Jabbok for me today. I'm all alone, for even though Tom will go to doctor's visits with me and feed me ice chips if I have surgery, he can't fix this. Nor can he go with me if I have to leave the earth early. I'm alone in this. And I've no other choice but to hurl myself on the mercy of God and hold tight, refusing to let go until He blesses me.

What presses you into your wrestling match with God? Is it a prodigal child? Your husband's addiction to pornography? Your own addiction to alcohol? Do you have cancer too? Or lupus or arthritis or Alzheimer's? Does your mother? Are you infertile? Lonely? Depressed or angry? No matter what presses you into the arms of God, I am certain you will hear His voice there. Hold on tight and don't let go. Remember, God loves this holy war.

Two Different Kinds of Wrestling

There are two different kinds of wrestling we enter with God. One is the kind that begs us to hold on tight until God gives His blessing, and the other is the kind that comes when we refuse to let go of our own agendas, our own solutions, and our own rights and ambitions. That kind of wrestling becomes a tug-of-war. And when you play tug-of-war with God, two things are going to happen: God's gonna win, and you might be dragged through the mud in the process.

I have to confess that I have done some kind of tug-of-war wrestling with God. It's tricky! I think I'm wrestling like Jacob to hang on until God blesses me . . . but instead I'm wrestling with wanting God to do things my way! The following is a blog post I shared a few winters ago. In it, I try to describe this wrong kind of wrestling.

My "Fight" With God

If you've been reading my blog for the past several months, you know that I'm praying through the darkest valley of my life. In this valley I've learned that the battle I'm fighting really has two fronts. One is the obvious one with the circumstances that are breaking my heart, and the other is with God.

That's right . . . my spiritual warfare includes my own personal struggle in my relationship with God. I'm not struggling with loving Him. Nor do I struggle with serving Him. But I do struggle with His sovereignty in this situation.

Every step of the way I've defined the reasonable boundaries of the other battlefront. For instance, I tell God what lines the Enemy must not be allowed to cross. I started doing this in June. But soon after I defined the boundary line, the Enemy crossed it. I was devastated. Then, last month, I defined another boundary with a deadline. The Enemy blasted over that boundary too.

Today I'm tempted to define two more boundary lines. My struggle with God has been unnecessarily magnified by these boundary lines. Once I define the boundaries, I decide that I know better than God how much is too much and how long is too long. When I do that I totally disregard God's Word in Isaiah 55:9: "As the heavens are higher than the earth, so are my ways higher than your ways and my thoughts than your thoughts."

The boundaries I construct become like barbed wire. They hem me in when I pray. I camp out just this side of them and spend much of my energy begging God to keep them strong. Thus far, those boundaries have been blatantly disregarded by the Enemy, and when he plows through them he drags me behind him. Often I'm left on the other side of that barbed wire, bleeding and wounded, wondering where God was when I just got taken further than I ever wanted to go into the depths of this valley.

But today I've decided to stop marking off the territory. I'm finally ready to say to God, "Wherever you want to go; and whatever you want to do, take me there and do that. As the heavens are higher than the earth, so are your ways higher than mine and your thoughts higher than my thoughts. You know what you're up to, and I trust you."

In order to wrestle with God like Jacob did, you have to let go of the details. You have to stop telling God *how* to bless you and simply insist that you will not turn loose of Him until He does. God's blessings come differently than we might anticipate. Paul reminded the church at Ephesus that God typically does "exceedingly abundantly more" than we can even think to ask! (Ephesians 3:20).

Wrestling With God Changes You

So often we come to God in prayer begging Him to change someone else. In fact, our most fervent prayers—the ones we are most anxious for Him to answer—almost always have to do with God changing someone else. It's funny how we are patient with God's work on us—and grateful that He is long-suffering—but when we want someone else to change, we want God to take care of them quickly.

Jacob wanted God to change Esau. He wanted God to make Esau a different man from the one he fled from twenty years earlier. Jacob wanted his family to be safe. He wanted to embrace all that God had promised would be his when God gave Jacob the dream with the ladder. This is understandable. I want what Jacob wanted too. But when Jacob wrestled with God, it wasn't Esau who was changed, it was Jacob. Don't miss this valuable truth. When you wrestle with God, He changes you!

> The man asked him, "What is your name?"
>
> "Jacob," he answered.
>
> Then the man said, "Your name will no longer be Jacob, but Israel, because you have struggled with God and with humans and have overcome."
>
> Genesis 32:27–28

Jacob's name meant "he grasps the heel or deceives." It was the name his parents gave him, and he certainly lived up to its meaning. But when Jacob took hold of God, God took hold of Jacob. The divine wrestling match changed Jacob so completely that the old man was gone and the new had come (2 Corinthians 5:17). God changed his name. Jacob would no longer be called "the one who deceives" but rather Israel, "the one who struggles with God."

I love the fact that God chose *Israel* to be the name that stayed with His people. He could have chosen Abraham. Abraham was a man of great faith. He had an intimate relationship with God and was the first to enter into a covenant relationship with Him. He was the first man to walk in that covenant relationship with God. It would have made sense for God to call His people Abraham. (We are going to talk more about Abraham in the next chapter.) God could have chosen Isaac. Isaac was the child of promise. He was tied to an altar and about to be sacrificed when God saved him from certain death at the hands of his father. Isaac understood obedience, surrender, and sacrifice. But God didn't choose Abraham or Isaac. He chose Jacob . . .

. . . the deceiver . . . the manipulator . . . the coward.

God chose Jacob, the one who was willing to take hold of God and refuse to let go. When God changed Jacob's name to Israel and chose Israel to be the name for His people, God declared to all of us that following Him would be a struggle, but if we hold tight in the struggle, He would bless us.

God chooses to be involved in your life. He wants you to take hold of Him and cling tight until you have His blessing.

The Progression of Jacob's Understanding of God

As Jacob lived a life of conflict, he grew in his understanding of his relationship with God. Look at the progression of Jacob's relationship with God over the course of his life.

Bethel: the house of God.

In Genesis 28:16–18, when Jacob was on the run from Esau, he met God personally in a dream and he felt like a guest in God's house. (Remember: *Bethel* means "house of God.")

> When Jacob awoke from his sleep, he thought, "Surely the Lord is in this place, and I was not aware of it." He was afraid and said, "How awesome is this place! This is none other than *the house of God*; this is the gate of heaven." Early the next morning Jacob took the stone he had placed under his head and set it up as a pillar and poured oil on top of it. He called that place Bethel.
>
> Genesis 28:16–19

Jacob left the safety and security of living in his parents' home. He was literally running for his life when God met him in a dream. Upon awakening, Jacob was convinced that somehow in his mad dash from home he had stumbled into "the house of God."

Peniel: the face of God.

In Genesis 32:30, after years of wrestling with Laban, Jacob wrestled with God and now knew Him intimately. Jacob was no longer a guest in God's house. Now he was an intimate companion with God. (*Peniel* means "face of God.")

> So Jacob called the place Peniel, saying, "It is because *I saw God face to face*, and yet my life was spared."
>
> Genesis 32:30

After Jacob's wrestling match he knew he'd had a powerful and personal encounter with God. Be careful not to miss the invitation to see God face-to-face when you take hold of God in a divine wrestling match.

El Bethel: God of his house.

And finally, after Jacob experienced God's protection and provision (Esau greeted Jacob as a brother and their relationship was mended), in Genesis 35:6–7 Jacob came back to the very place he started. This time, He understood that God was not only in this "sacred place," but that God was also with Jacob everywhere he had been. Jacob also understood that God would be with him everywhere he would go. God was OVER the "house" in Bethel, not merely in it. God was also in Haran with Laban, He was in Sier with Esau, in Shechem with Jacob, and no matter where Jacob went or what difficulties he encountered . . . God was there. (*El Bethel* means "God of His House.")

> Jacob and all the people with him came to Luz (that is, Bethel) in the land of Canaan. There he built an altar, and he called the place *El Bethel, because it was there that God revealed himself to him* when he was fleeing from his brother.

God and Jesus and Me—We're Gonna Wrestle!

I don't know where you might be in your journey with God. You may be where Jacob was when he laid his head on that rock. You might be living year number eleven of twenty, waiting on God to fulfill His promise to you. Or you might be at the ford of the Jabbok, facing the only thing that stands between you and God's promise to you, eager for Him to remove that final obstacle. No matter where you are, know this: God will use the circumstances you find yourself in today to reveal himself to you. You will grow in your understanding of Him. You will move from a place of casual acquaintance to intimate companion if you will take hold of Him and wrestle hard.

Are you wrestling with God? Would you dare? Which kind of wrestling are you engaged in? A "tug-of-war" or a "hanging on tight"?

When my daughter Mikel was four, she loved to wrestle with her daddy. He would come home from work and lie on the living room floor. Soon all three of our little people would jump up and down all over him. He'd toss them to the floor; they'd squeal and giggle. They'd jump up and straddle his back; he'd rear his head like a horse and whinny real loud. They would slide off his back and roll underneath him. They would carry on like this until Tom got tired—or I called a time-out.

Mikel loved this. We were in the minivan on our way to church one Wednesday night when Mikel said, "Mommy, you want to know what I'm gonna do when I get to heaven?"

"No, what?" I asked, impressed that she sounded as matter-of-fact about heaven as she did about church or the grocery store.

"God and Jesus and me—we're gonna wrestle!" Mikel exclaimed.

I smiled because to her, wrestling with her father was so much fun that in her preschool heart and mind she knew that wrestling with God and Jesus would be the same. Just imagine, wrestling with your heavenly Father, grabbing hold of all He has in store for you and clinging on for dear life, embracing His promises and holding them tight, knowing beyond a shadow of a doubt that He is making a way for you!

If you are living with disappointment, tragedy, or crisis—and these things seem to mock God's promise to you—know that God is honored when we wrestle with Him. God invites us to wrestle with Him today, most often through prayer. Don't be timid, don't be afraid! Approach the throne of grace with confidence, pray with the authority of His powerful name, and hang on tight until He blesses you.

Treasure Hunt

Personal Reflections

- Read Jacob's story again in Genesis 27–33 and 35.
- Has God given you any promises? Are some of His promises waiting to be fulfilled? Which ones?
- Jot down the desires of your heart that look to you like the fulfillment of God's promises.
- Write the promise God gave you. This will be a passage of Scripture related to your desires.

Discussion Questions

1. What would you have thought of Jacob had you met him just after he ran from home?
2. If you were one of Rachel or Leah's brothers, would you have been surprised that God chose to name a nation after him?
3. Have you ever been pressed forward by your faith and pressed back by your fear? If so, would you share that with the group?
4. Share a time in your life when you took hold of God and He blessed you.

Treasure Verse

Then the man said, "Your name will no longer be Jacob, but Israel, because you have struggled with God and with humans and have overcome."

Genesis 32:28

4

Abraham's Story Begins

The Lord had said to Abram, "Go from your country, your people and your father's household to the land I will show you. I will make you into a great nation, and I will bless you; I will make your name great, and you will be a blessing. I will bless those who bless you, and whoever curses you I will curse; and all peoples on earth will be blessed through you."

Genesis 12:1–3

We hear God's voice when we press in to His promises and refuse to let go. With Jacob's wrestling match fresh on your mind, I want to take you back a bit in history to the story of his grandfather, Abraham. While Abraham didn't actually *wrestle* with God physically like Jacob did, he did struggle for many years with hearing and understanding God's voice as related to the gap that existed between God's promise and Abraham's reality. It was twenty years between God's promise to Jacob and its fulfillment. For Abraham it was much longer than that. In fact, there was a season in Abraham's consistent (and might I add faithful) walk with God when God was silent for thirteen years (see Genesis 16:16 and 17:1). Imagine if you had to suffer God's silence for thirteen years. Abraham did just that, and he's heralded as both the father of our faith and a man whose faith serves as an example to us today (see Hebrews 11). But don't worry, I'm not going to write this chapter on God's silence.

Instead, in these next three chapters I'm going to take you on a walk through Abraham's life so that you can see his faith grow. As Abraham's faith grew, his ability to hear and understand the voice of God increased. What began as Abraham's confidence in a picture developed into his assurance of God's promise and finally evolved into his trust in a Person. As you read Abraham's story, consider the journey of faith that God has invited you to take.

Abraham's life gives us a great picture of how we ought to manage our lives in the "meantime." In the past several years, I've changed *meantime* to *mean* time in my own vocabulary. For there is not much that I consider *nice* about the time that I have to live in between God's promises and the fulfillment of them. However, the time that I call *mean* is the same time that God calls a *walk of faith*. And He uses Abraham (and Sarah, and Noah, and others) to describe it.

> All these people were still living by faith when they died. They did not receive the things promised; they only saw them and welcomed them from a distance, admitting that they were foreigners and strangers on earth.
>
> Hebrews 11:13

Listen for the voice of God as He speaks to you through Abraham's story.

Pictures, Dreams, and Other Things

When we wrestle with God, we tend to have a picture of what we want Him to do. Mrs. Anna's mama explained that the wrestling match itself was directly linked to some sort of confusion over what

God was (or was not) doing in relationship to our preconceived notions. We have vivid imaginations, and we learn to use them at a very young age. And while some of our dreams are of our own making, others are planted by God.

When I was twenty years old I spent the summer in the rural parts of Nevada. I don't know if you've ever been to Nevada, or if you live there now, but if you have or if you do, you know that rural Nevada redefines rural. Besides jackrabbits and sagebrush, there is not much there. I felt much like Moses when he spent his forty years in the wilderness and then stumbled upon the burning bush, where he heard God's voice loud and clear. Only I spent ten weeks in the desert of Nevada and never saw a burning bush. But I did hear the voice of God loud and clear.

One thing rural Nevada had was incredible sunsets. It was as if God's canvas were stretched across the sky, and each evening He painted an original piece just for me. While watching His master-piece unfold, I talked with God. I thanked Him for the sunset and then I began to tell Him all about my dreams. I wanted a good man to be my life's companion, one who loved God and wanted to serve Him. I hoped to have children someday so I could experience being a mother. But mostly I wanted to matter to God's kingdom. I wanted to serve Him and use the gifts He put in me to impact eternity. I asked God if that meant that I was to dedicate myself to "full-time vocational service" (a phrase used often among Christian teens in my growing-up years). I don't remember how He said it, but somehow during that summer I knew that God had "called" me to give my life full-time to His kingdom work.

My stepping-on place was much like Abraham's. I had already gone to a land I knew nothing about (rural Nevada), and I looked forward to going wherever God wanted me to go after college. When I met Tom at Southwestern Seminary, where we were getting our Master's degrees, he fit all that I'd imagined my husband to be. We married during the Christmas break that came at the halfway point of our seminary training. But when we graduated from seminary in Texas and moved to Tennessee, I was ready for children, and my babies didn't come. It was the first time I wrestled with God. And wrestle I did—in good form (Jacob would've been proud)—but unlike Abram, my waiting time was only three years. In 1992, 1993, and 1995 God blessed me with those babies. He gave me three answers to my heart cries: two daughters, Mikel and Kaleigh, and one son, TJ.

Tom and I spent years building a great church, serving our denomination in leadership roles, and writing and speaking. Finally, the picture God had given me unfolded with my first book deal with a big publisher, and I wrote a "real" book. (I'm not sure what I call the other seven books I've written; I guess they're real too.) As I wrote my book on spiritual warfare, I braced for attack. I had cancer and our church experienced a flood, and we were shaken but not destroyed. But when my daughter left us and chose her boyfriend over all that I'd imagined God had in store for her life, my picture of what life should be was ripped to shreds.

In my weakest moments of grief the summer I was writing that book, I even cried out to God that I was sorry I'd ever taken it on. Is it okay to be that honest with you here? I might have felt differently if she hadn't been "the answer" to my infertility prayers. *She* was the one I prayed for! *She* was the one I committed to the Lord three years before she was ever conceived. *Her* husband was the man I'd prayed for since the minute I discovered I was pregnant with her. *She* was the one that God had promised to be "mighty to save" when we first started losing her to what we considered a very bad relationship with a very questionable young man.

Today she is a member of the "Silent Ranks" (the designation that spouses of military personnel give themselves). Her boyfriend is now my son-in-law, and he's a soldier in the U.S. army. I'm proud of the profession he's chosen and the provision he's making for his family. She and my granddaughter live in a home near their post in Clarksville, Tennessee.

I'm sharing this with you just to let you know that while I haven't wandered in Canaan for decades (like Abraham did), I have bumbled about in Tennessee for a whole lot of days, wondering if God remembers what He promised me before she was born.

Abram's Picture of God's Promise

In Genesis 12 God called Abram. He told him to go to a place that he knew nothing about. But He assured Abram that as he went, God himself would make Abram into a great nation. Let's stop right there (because God promised several other great things too, but this is the one that created the picture that invited Abram into his wrestling match with God).

At this point in Abram's story, God hadn't changed his name. *Abram* meant "exalted father." When God changed Abram's name, he took "exalted father" and twisted it to become *Abraham,* "father of a multitude." I find it interesting that Abram had a picture in his mind of being a father before God ever spoke to him. For as long as Abram could remember, he was always called "exalted father." Because names were linked to destiny in the Old Testament culture, if Abram understood anything, it was that he was destined to be a father.

A funny little sideline I found interesting is that Abram's brothers were named Nahor and Haran. Want to know what their names mean? *Nahor* means "snorting," and *Haran* means "mountaineer." Hmm . . . Nonetheless, Abram, the eldest of Terah's boys, was named "exalted father." Even his own dad, Terah (which means "wanderer"), had a picture in mind for Abram's life. I can totally relate to that! How many of us mothers have beautiful pictures in mind for our children? By the time we discover their gender at the ultrasound appointment, we already have them dating the choicest people, going to the right schools, curing cancer, and singing solos in the church choir.

But not all our dreams come true. Although Abram did marry the right girl and live in close community with his family, consider the constant pain Abram might have had knowing that his father longed for him to be a father. But in reality he suffered infertility with his wife. Every time anyone spoke to him he was reminded:

"Exalted father," how was the quail hunt?
"Exalted father," do you like your steak medium or rare?
"Exalted father," meet me after work for dinner at the Ur Café.

I know what infertility feels like, although I only experienced it for a few years. Tom and I still shed tears when we see infertility portrayed in television dramas. I can only imagine what it must be like for those who've dealt with it for many years, and for those who are never able to conceive children. Infertility is a difficult journey to walk—one that shouts emptiness, longing, and despair. Abram and Sarai knew what infertility felt like. While imagining afternoons of hunting with his sons and evenings of sharing meals with his daughters, Abram most likely struggled with God's word to him.

"Come on, Abram! Come with me to a strange land and I'm going to make you into a nation!" God declared (see Genesis 12:1–2).

Abram might have responded, "Wouldn't I have to have a son in order to be the father of a nation? Maybe a few sons? What part of 'We've got no children' are you missing?" There's no biblical evidence that Abram was thinking these thoughts—not at this point in the story anyway. But because I've been there and done that, I kind of think he might have had a few of these questions bouncing about in his head—and if not there, certainly in his heart.

So why, if God intended to make a nation out of Abram, was Sarai infertile? Was God messing with him?

Listen to what my friend Julie said. This is the same Julie who prayed for my spiritual spelunking. She was leading worship at one of our twenty-four hours of prayer and praise, and it was early on

Saturday morning. There were fewer than ten people in the room when Julie stopped singing and simply said, "God doesn't *mess* with you."

Let that sink in for a minute.

God doesn't mess with you!

If He's given you a picture anchored in a promise, he will not heckle you with it. God intends to do what He has promised. I don't know when, and I don't know how, but I know that I know that I know that God always keeps His promises. I love how Job put it: The plans of the Lord will not be thwarted (42:2).

I think I like that verse because I like the word *thwarted*. Say it out loud—sounds good, doesn't it?

Several times the men and women we read about in the Bible might have thought God was messing with them. Abram could have been one of them. God gave Abram more than a promise; He changed his name. God took "exalted father" and redefined his destiny . . . made it more definitive by changing *Abram* to *Abraham*, "father of a multitude." (He changed Sarai's name too. Where her name once meant "princess," God changed her name to *Sarah*, which means "princess of a multitude.") But all the while, the "father of a multitude" and the "princess of a multitude" remained infertile.

God does not heckle you with His promises. He keeps them— every one. If there's any heckling going on, you can be sure the devil—not God—is behind it. And oh, how Satan loves to heckle us with the promises of God.

Hearing the Voice of God

This book is about hearing the voice of God. So let me make this absolutely clear. Many times we hear the voice of God clearly. The

61

things He tells us sync up perfectly with the desires He planted in our hearts. But because our present circumstances don't reflect what we heard, and our hearts are breaking over the gulf that exists between what we heard and the reality of what we're living with, we let the heckling of the Enemy drown out the voice of God. Rather than stand firm on what we know we heard, we question and fret and get all confused over what does not make sense.

Your *mean* time is sure to be infested with hecklers. But no matter how much those voices of darkness heckle you, stand firm on the fact that it makes no sense at all for God *not* to keep His word to you. If you are tempted to think that God has let you down—that in your particular situation He will prove unfaithful—I want you to stop right there and take it to the cross. Why would God, who proved His love for you by sending His very own Son to die a cruel death on the cross, set you up to expect great things from Him just to let you down?

He won't. Romans 8:32 tells you what to say in response to your hecklers. Say this,

> He who did not spare his own Son, but gave him up for us all—how will he not also, along with him, graciously give us all things?

Therefore, stick to what you heard God say. Hold tight to it. And when the devil comes near to heckle you, wrap your arms around the foot of the splintery old cross and sing this song—and sing it loud.

"Jesus loves me THIS I know . . ."

Why Does God Do This to Us?

Throughout Scripture we read the stories of men and women who followed God right into a mess.

Consider Joseph. God gave him a dream of his sheaf of wheat rising up and his brothers' sheaves bowing down to his. Joseph shared his dream with his brothers, and they hated him for it. Then he had another dream. Only this time the sun, moon, and eleven stars were all bowing down to him! His father even rebuked him for this dream when he shared it with his family (Genesis 37). I've no doubt at all that Joseph carried a picture of greatness in his heart from the moment he had those dreams. What must he have thought when his brothers tossed him into a pit, then sold him into slavery? I've written more about Joseph in chapter 7 of this book. For now, just know that years of disappointment separated Joseph from his dreams.

And what about Moses? Reluctantly and for LOTS of reasons, he wasn't the best one for the job—Moses surrendered to God's call on his life and partnered with God in freeing the Israelites from Pharaoh. After doing everything that God told him to do, Moses led the Israelites out of Egypt only to find himself with a sea in front of him and an army behind him. What must Moses have felt in that moment? (Exodus 14).

Consider Joshua. Quaking in his sandals, he bowed under the heavy yoke of leadership that was placed on him—having to follow in the footsteps of Moses, one of Israel's greatest leaders of all time. Joshua tried hard to calm his beating heart with God's tremendous promise, "Be strong and courageous. Do not be afraid; do not be discouraged, for the Lord your God will be with you wherever you go" (Joshua 1:9). But there he stood on a bloody battlefield—even after being promised victory over his enemy at Gibeon. The sun was setting and victory was not secure. How did Joshua feel? (Joshua 10).

What about Esther? After being chosen as queen to the king of Persia, she discovered that all of her people were to be destroyed by the wicked Haman. She was obedient and loyal and certainly didn't consider herself a savior. But God had put her in a place where she had to choose whether to intervene for her people at the risk of her life, or sit idly by and watch them die—would God abandon her now?

The list could go on and on and on . . . for each of these followers of God, there was a time and a place when they might have wondered if God was messing with them. The other day God gave me a thought. It was actually a question with an obvious answer. I read somewhere recently that when God asks us questions it's not to discover the answer—it's just to hear what we say. Here was God's question to me: "Leighann, was I any less God the second year of Joseph's long imprisonment than I was when Joseph was put in charge of Egypt?" (Genesis 39:19–41:41).

Think about that. Was He? No! And He's no less God in the midst of our trials. It's just easier to see God's hand in the lives of these biblical heroes because we're looking from the other side of the completed story of their lives. God is the same yesterday, today, and tomorrow. In fact, God exists above and beyond time, so He is living in yesterday, today, and tomorrow all at the same time! He is worthy of your praise and your thanksgiving because He already lives where your prayers are answered.

Unlike the men and woman that I've mentioned above, God's still writing your story! If God has given you a picture (or a name or a promise or an ark), you can be SURE He's going to PAINT IT!

My Picture of My Children's Futures

I went to a small Christian college in a city near my home. My parents wanted me to attend a small college, and I never questioned their desire. I simply looked at a few good schools and chose one. So when it came time to search for colleges for my girls, we did what my parents did. We visited several small Christian colleges in our area and invited them to choose one.

Tom went where the money was. He chose his college based on the financial aid that was offered; his education could be paid for. So when one of the schools offered huge scholarship packages to our daughters, our decisions were made and the plan was that they would go to that fine school and receive a cost-effective, quality education.

You know what Mikel chose—but listen to what happened to Kaleigh. Kaleigh went to the college that offered the scholarships and tried hard to make it work. But halfway through her freshman year she was beginning to feel like a caged animal. Her heart cried out to make a difference in the real world. But the code of conduct and rules that helped to create the Christian environment at her school squelched her inner drive to stretch her wings and fly. So she decided to change schools. Now Kaleigh is at the University of Tennessee—with all its alcohol and promiscuity and foul language and big city.

My picture of my children's future is starting to look a whole lot different from the one I took for granted when they were twelve. I share this to make this point: Sometimes what we think might be God's promise to us is, in reality, our own imagination. I understood God's promise that my children will embrace the faith and live Christ-centered lives, but then I added details to that promise. I thought, *Since they are going to live Christ-centered lives, my daughters will go to small Christian colleges; they will marry godly men and have sweet little babies and live in peaceful homes.* See what I did? I allowed my own imagination to paint various pictures and included them in God's promise.

I had a friend who told me one day that if I was going to trust God to paint the picture, I needed to step away from the canvas. When your idea of what ought to be happening doesn't come about, you might be adding details to a work of art that God is capable of completing on His own. God is not obligated to fulfill your plans. His plans are the ones He's promised to bring about.

Do you have a picture in mind of how the fulfillment of God's promise might look? I would imagine that during Sarah's child-bearing years Abraham anticipated her pregnancy. After all, to father a nation he'd have to father a child. But every month Sarah remained barren, and after years of trying, she and Abraham most likely gave up. They were too old to have children of their own, so they thought.

Treasure Hunt

Personal Reflections

- Are you too old? Have you waited too long? What is God saying to you in this *mean* time? What was God's original promise to you? What has it become in your mind?

Discussion Questions

1. Consider giving each group member a piece of paper and some crayons. Encourage each one to draw pictures that represent the "something" they long for God to do in their lives. Emphasize that this isn't an art project—no one's judging the picture. It's just a way of putting on paper what is in her heart.
2. Share your pictures if you are willing.
3. Discuss the promises that God has given you related to what your pictures represent.

Treasure Verse

Then Job replied to the Lord: "I know that you can do all things; no purpose of yours can be thwarted."

Job 42:1–2

5

All God's Promises Are YES!

For no matter how many promises God has made, they are "Yes" in Christ. And so through Him the "Amen" is spoken by us to the glory of God.

2 Corinthians 1:20

God speaks boldly through His Word. And in the Bible God graciously gives us promises galore. Every one of God's promises are faithful and true. Not only that, but each of them are for you. Most people who profess to be Christians don't even take the time to claim them as their own. I applaud you and your faith because you are one of the rare disciples who actually believes that God's promises were meant for you. And they are. All of them!

Abram understood that God had given him a "word." Abram heard God's word, so he walked daily in awareness of God's promise and in expectation that God would make good on His word. But as he walked, he encountered various trials. Some of those trials Abram conquered like a great man of faith, and some he failed miserably. As we take a look at Abram's trials, let the lesson of his life be to take care along the way. Be careful as you sojourn through your *mean* time not to lose faith simply because life gets tough.

Remember in chapter 1 how I told you that God most often speaks to us in His Word? The Bible will always tell you the truth. Sometimes the problem with our faith is not that we don't hear God's voice, but that we perhaps don't like what He is saying. Consider this honest statement straight out of God's Word:

> He causes his sun to rise on the evil and the good, and sends rain on the righteous and the unrighteous.
>
> Matthew 5:45

Many times we struggle in our faith, thinking that we're missing something because it happens to be a rainy day (or season) in our lives. Rather than question your faith or your ability to hear and understand God's voice, recognize that He's capable of keeping His promises even in the rain. In this chapter we will take a look at some of Abram's "rainy days" and how God used them to solidify His promise.

Abram and the Famine

Abram responded to God's call to leave his country, his people, and his father's family, and went to Canaan. While Abram was sitting under a tree, God told him that this was the land He was giving to Abram. Abram roamed around looking at his land for a while, and then there was a famine (Genesis 12:5–10).

What about that? Abram followed God, obeyed Him, and trusted Him, and not only was his wife infertile, but now his "promised" land was as well. Because of this famine, Abram headed to Egypt, where the famine was not so bad. Once he got there he took matters in his own hands and twisted the truth. He didn't actually lie, because Sarai really was his half sister. (I don't even want to go there in this book; just suffice it to say that things were very different in Abram's day than they are today.) Abram implied that his relationship with Sarai was that of brother and sister, and because Sarai was beautiful (I love that part because it starts sounding like the princess stories to me), Pharaoh claimed her as his own. That didn't work out too well because God intervened. Remember Job 42:2?

The purpose of the Lord will not be thwarted.

God planned to make Abram a "father of a multitude" and Sarai a "princess of a multitude," and He didn't intend for Pharaoh's blood to get in the mix. So God caused disease to spread to Pharaoh's household, and Pharaoh heard the voice of God.

So Pharaoh summoned Abram. "What have you done to me?" he said. "Why didn't you tell me she was your wife? Why did you say, 'She is my sister,' so that I took her to be my wife? Now then, here is your wife. Take her and go!"

Genesis 12:18–19

Abram and Lot

So Abram left Egypt and headed up to the Negev. There he and Lot were blessed with such prosperity that conflict erupted between Lot's herdsmen and Abram's. Note that it was God's blessing that led to the conflict. Sometimes this happens in our lives too. The blessings that God pours out on us can create conflict with family and/or friends. If you have been blessed with prosperity, you will be less likely to relate well to family members who are struggling financially. If you receive a call on your life similar to the call Abram had on his, and you eagerly follow God to an unknown land, you might run into conflict with well-meaning family and friends who don't want you to go. In these ways the blessing of God actually contributes to the conflict. Such was the case for Abram and Lot.

But they settled their conflict, and Abram demonstrated great faith in God (and humility in relationship with Lot) by giving his nephew his choice of the land. Because of this, God spoke to Abram again and reassured him that he was going to inherit more land than he could imagine, and that all of what he inherited from God would be passed down to his offspring. God even invited Abram to walk about and explore his land (see Genesis 13).

Later Abram rescued Lot and the people of Sodom from foreign invasion. Because of his victory, the king of Sodom wanted to honor Abram, but Abram gave all the credit to God and refused the king's gifts. Once again his humility captured God's attention.

> The word of the Lord came to Abram in a vision: "Do not be afraid, Abram. I am your shield, your very great reward."
>
> Genesis 15:1

This is where Abram's story gets good. Abram's problem wasn't hearing God's voice, but rather trusting what he heard. Over and over God promised Abram land and a nation. But thus far all Abram has experienced is famine, conflict, and increasing livestock. This is where he gets gut-level honest with God.

A Reasonable Question and a Great Response

> But Abram said, "Sovereign Lord, what can you give me since I remain childless and the one who will inherit my estate is Eliezer of Damascus?" And Abram said, "You have given me no children; so a servant in my household will be my heir."
>
> Genesis 15:2–3

Can I paraphrase this for us? "Lord, I know that you are my shield and I want to know that you are my very great reward, but a long time ago you promised me that you'd make me a father of a nation. And yet today—after ample time for you to give me some children—I still don't have any. What about *that* promise, Lord? Are you still going to make good on that one?"

After following God faithfully for many years and wandering all over the great land that God promised him, Abram was ready to experience the rest of God's blessing. I would have been too. Wouldn't you? God was patient with Abram's frustration and rewarded his honesty with a great response:

> Then the word of the Lord came to him: "This man will not be your heir, but a son who is your own flesh and blood will be your heir." He took him outside and said, "Look up at the sky and count the stars—if indeed you can count them." Then he said to him, "So shall your offspring be."
>
> Genesis 15:4–5

Isn't that great? If you are tired of waiting, if you are serving God faithfully, and if you walk in humility in relationship to God and to others in the *mean* time, then consider getting gut-level honest with Him. Tell God how you feel and what bothers you most about the breach between His promise and your reality. If you do this, and then listen closely for God to respond, you just might get an invitation to go star gazing.

The best part of this entire story is the very next verse in Genesis 15:

> Abram believed the Lord, and he credited it to him as righteousness.

Abram took God at His word. He trusted Him and believed, and when Abram believed, God smiled and said yes, for He knew that He had reached right down into the heart of a sin-stained man and drawn him into a personal, dynamic (living and active) relationship with himself.

After that, Abram and God had an interesting experience together involving a heifer, a goat, and a ram, each three years old, as well as a dove and a young pigeon. We're not going to go into all that, but it would have been recorded as a spiritual highlight in Abram's life. For it was a sign of the covenant between God and Abram that was understood in Abram's culture; kind of like contracts are to us today (Genesis 15:7–21).

The Biggest Trial of All—Taking Matters Into His Own Hands

Abram walked away from his powerful encounter with God, knowing a bit more about God and a bit more about himself. But just as happens to many of us, his spiritual high was matched by a spiritual low. We tend to forget that Abram's *mean* time was Sarai's *mean* time too. And true to form, because we women are so good at this, Sarai came up with a plan to help God out. Obviously God needed her help, and His plans just might be thwarted if she didn't intervene. (At least that's what I think she was thinking, because it's what I would have thought.)

So Sarai presented her maidservant, Hagar, to Abram with the hopes of building a family through her. It must have been their culture's version of a surrogate mother. Only after Hagar got pregnant, she considered herself better than Sarai (that's pretty typical of women too), and Sarai grew to hate her. Abram, not wanting to get in the middle of this madness, simply told Sarai to do whatever she wanted with Hagar, and so Sarai mistreated her.

Can you believe all this? Is this really the man whose faith we were presented as an example for our own? And did God really choose Sarai to be the "princess of a multitude"? She doesn't sound like a homecoming queen to me.

Anyway, things got so bad that Hagar ran away and an angel served as the first counselor ever of a crisis pregnancy center. The angel met Hagar and ministered to her, and then sent her back to her home to have her son. I do think that it's a very sweet twist in this story that Ishmael's name means "God hears." That is the name given by God to the child who was born out of all this mess. Ishmael's name tells me that there's not a woman in the world who can thwart the plans of God, nor is there one who can out-sin God's willingness to forgive. Not only that, but there is also not one single child conceived in sin that God doesn't love.

When God's Word Remains the Same

Abram was eighty-six years old when Ishmael was born. Thirteen years went by with no word from God. Then suddenly, when Abram was ninety-nine years old, the Lord appeared to him and spoke again. This time He said what He had continually said before,

I am God Almighty; walk with me and be blameless.

Genesis 17:1

Oh my! Had God held Abram's sin against him all these years? Why did He begin His conversation with those words? Here is something you need to know if you are serious about wanting to hear God's voice: God is serious about sin . . . dead serious. While we might get comfortable in our lives of compromise, God never does. There's no indication that Abram ever went to God and asked Him to forgive him for taking matters into his own hands (or rather letting Sarai take matters into her own hands). Perhaps God greeted Abram with these words because He wanted Abram to understand that He will not tolerate compromise or watered-down obedience.

I'm almost certain that the reason so many of us have such a hard time hearing God's voice is that we want Him to bless our namby-pamby faith walks. We are not serious enough about honoring His holiness to pursue holiness in our everyday lives. In fact, we're more concerned about what He is or isn't doing to bless us than we are about what we are or are not doing to honor Him. If this is the case for you, listen closely to God's word for you today (it's His word to me as I write this):

I am God Almighty; walk before me faithfully and be blameless.

Back to Abram and his conversation with God.

I am God Almighty; walk before me faithfully and be blameless. Then I will make my covenant between me and you and will greatly increase your numbers.

Genesis 17:1–2

Isn't that great? After His rebuke and command, God assured Abram that even though he chose disobedience and compromise, God would reconfirm His covenant with him. I love this. It tells me that God has already taken into account the fact that I will disappoint Him. And His promises to me are not contingent on my ability to impress Him with my impeccable behavior. God doesn't necessarily reward us when we're good and punish us when we're bad. He simply gives us an abundance of promises rooted in His own character, goodness, and passion for us, and He makes good on them based on His own merit, not ours.

That doesn't mean that we can excuse ourselves from living lives pleasing to Him. No! In fact, He tells us multiple times in His Word that He expects us to strive toward holiness (see Hebrews 12:14). But even when we fail, God doesn't dismiss us and kick us out of the kingdom. Instead He lovingly rebukes us and reconfirms His commitment to us.

This is the moment when God changed Abram's name to Abraham (Genesis 17:5). He went on to tell Abraham that he would be very fruitful, and that the covenant relationship He's established with Abraham would be passed on to his descendants. God initiated circumcision as a sign of the covenant relationship that Abraham and his family shared with God. And then He explained very clearly that Sarai (not Hagar, nor any other of Sarai's great ideas) would be the mother of the son that God intended to give Abraham.

After God was done talking, you would think that Abraham would lay prostrate before the Lord Almighty, beg for His forgiveness, and maybe even set up a rock and anoint it with oil. But no!

> Abraham fell facedown; he laughed and said to himself, "Will a son be born to a man a hundred years old? Will Sarah bear a child at the age of ninety?" And Abraham said to God, "If only Ishmael might live under your blessing!"
>
> Genesis 17:17–18

How about that? What an interesting prayer! The super-spiritual part of me wants to hide behind a bush and gasp at Abraham's audacity to doubt the word of God. But that's only because I know the rest of the story. For in my own life, I've often been guilty of the same kind of prayers. I water down what I originally expected God to do because so much time has separated me from when I first believed. I give God some "outs." I make it easy for Him so that He can just bless what is believable rather than do the impossible. For when God insists on doing the impossible, I feel like I have to defend His seeming silence in my life. But when Abraham fell over laughing, God never flinched, He just went right on.

Ishmael and God's Goodness

> Yes, . . .
>
> Genesis 17:19

Before we move forward, we have to stop right here. Notice what God just answered yes to. Abraham asked God to let Ishmael ("God hears") live under His blessing, and God said Y . . . E . . . S!

Isn't that great? Ishmael, the "oops child" in this story, just received the blessing of God. Through the years I've heard it taught that we suffer from Sarai's shenanigans because the Muslims of today trace their ancestry back to Ishmael as the father of their faith. I have actually taught that truth as a dire warning to women. I warn us that when we work to help God out, our actions have long-lasting consequences. And it is true, Islam is linked to Ishmael, and those who follow its teaching are definitely in desperate need of the same salvation that we know is found in Christ alone. But the curse that imbedded itself down the ranks of Ishmael's descendants was not planted by God. For in Genesis 17:19, God promised Abraham to bless the "we took matters into our own hands" child. And later when Abraham reluctantly cut Ishmael off from the blessing of his house, God himself took care of him (Genesis 21:20). When Abraham died an old man, Ishmael and Isaac buried their father together (Genesis 25:9).

He Who Laughs Last Laughs Most

I don't know if Abraham inspired God's decision to name his son Isaac, or if God planned to give him that name all along, but I like it. Let's get back to the story. Abraham fell facedown, laughed his head off at the thought of he and Sarah producing a child at their age, and asked God just to let Ishmael fulfill the promise. And this is what God said:

> Yes, but your wife Sarah will bear you a son, and you will call him Isaac.
>
> Genesis 17:19

"Yes, 'father of a multitude,' I will indeed bless Ishmael, but your wife, 'princess of a multitude,' will bear you a son and you will call him 'he laughs.'"

I think God has a great sense of humor! We still laugh when we tell this story. It was a fitting name for a miracle child.

God went on to explain how much He would bless both of Abraham's children, and how not only one but now two nations would come from his loins. Abraham circumcised his entire household in response to this conversation with God.

A little while later God sent three angels to visit with Abraham, and they announced that the time was now for Abraham's baby to be conceived. This time Sarah laughed and God chuckled.

Sometime after this Abraham had to have intercourse with Sarah. Have you thought about that? Do one-hundred-year-old men and ninety-year-old women still do that? I don't mention this to be trite, but to make the point that after all these years, Abraham and Sarah clung to God's promise enough to partner with Him in bringing it to fruition. They might have laughed, they might have cried, but somewhere at sometime, that very old couple had sex and conceived a son.

Treasure Hunt

Personal Reflection

- Take a few minutes to underline these verses in your Bible. Then answer the questions related to each one.

  2 Corinthians 1:20

  Psalm 145:13

  Numbers 23:19

Discussion Questions

1. 2 Corinthians 1:20
   - How many promises are YES?
   - *Amen* means "so be it." When we say "so be it" to the promises of God, what do we do?

- When do our lives reflect God's glory more? When things are going well, or when things are not going so well and we are shouting SO BE IT until it is good?
- Remember, ALL GOD'S PROMISES ARE YES!

2. Psalm 145:13 (That last part: The Lord is faithful to all His promises and loving toward all He has made.)
   - How many promises is the Lord faithful to?
   - What is God's attitude toward all that He has made?

3. Numbers 23:19
   - Will God ever lie to you?
   - Does He ever change His mind regarding His promises to you?
   - Does He say He'll do something and fail to do it?
   - Does He ever NOT keep a promise He's made to you?
   - How can we know that God will keep His promises?

     He tells us He will!

     He has never not kept a single promise He has ever made.

     He wouldn't be God if He didn't exist within the parameters of His Person. He is a PROMISE KEEPER!

Treasure Verse

For no matter how many promises God has made, they are "Yes" in Christ. And so through Him the "Amen" is spoken by us to the glory of God.

2 Corinthians 1:20

6

Abraham, You're the Man!

When they reached the place God had told him about, Abraham
built an altar there and arranged the wood on it. He bound his son
Isaac and laid him on the altar, on top of the wood. Then he reached
out his hand and took the knife to slay his son.

Genesis 22:9–10

Hopefully by now you understand that much of your ability to
hear God's voice is directly linked to discovering, understanding, and claiming the promises He's offered you in His Word. I've
provided a start to a list of God's promises in appendix 1. But don't
just take these promises from the page of my book and claim them
as your own. Take time to read them in the Bible in the context
that they were given. When you do this you will discover how God
works in the lives of people who trust Him.

Through the study of Abraham's life, I have learned that I
have to let go of the picture that my own imagination paints in
response to God's promise to me. I have also learned that when the
howling winds and the torrential rains come, I can tether myself
to God's Word (His promises). Tying myself to God's Word will
keep me from flying away. But there's one more thing I've learned

through the study of Abraham's life: There comes a time when I have to turn my attention from the promise and settle it instead on the Person who gave it. In this chapter you will discover what I mean by that.

One More Look at Genesis 15:6

Abram believed the Lord, and he credited it to him as righteousness.

Remember this moment? It was right after Abram explained to God that although God was certain that Abram would have children, Abram and his wife remained childless. It's really the first time that we see Abram being utterly honest with God in prayer.

Regarding this moment in Abram's life, Jennifer Kennedy Dean said:

The whole grand story from beginning to end turns on this moment when Abraham believed God, and God credited it to him as righteousness. . . .

Abraham believed God. The Hebrew verb suggests that Abraham entrusted himself to God as a child entrusts himself to his parent. God had made promises to Abraham before. Had Abraham not believed until now?

Abraham believed in the past. He had risked everything on his confidence in God's promise. But before, Abraham had believed God because what God promised was believable. God promised Abraham. Abraham evaluated the promise and said to himself, "Sure. That could happen." God promised Abraham a son. Abraham and Sarai were still in their childbearing years. That's believable. Abraham believed the promise.

Now the promise is no longer believable. The promise hinges on a son. Sarai is past the age of childbearing. Now Abraham does something different, he believes God. His faith rests in who God is—his shield and his very great reward. . . .

Abraham shifted his focus from the circumstances and fastened it on the Person who had the power to do what He promised. Faith flooded in. He received. He gave himself up to the living word of the living God and quit trying to evaluate and measure the circumstances to see if there was still a chance that God could come through. He stopped letting his own sense of what should be happening hinder him in his journey of faith. He let God deliver the promise at the appointed time. He received.[1]

When God credited it to Abraham as righteousness, it was because Abraham "believed God." Do you believe God?

Embrace the PERSON

In the previous chapter we discussed the story of Isaac's beginning. "He laughs" was born to Abraham and Sarah when Abraham was one hundred years old. Sarah survived labor and delivery, and everyone laughed with them (Genesis 21:1–7). I cannot even begin to imagine the saggy breast that fed Isaac, nor the joy that must have literally made Sarah tingle.

But that's not where Abraham's story ends; there's more. Turn in your Bible to Genesis 22:1–18. Just above Genesis 22 in my Bible I have this phrase: "Abraham Tested." Do you remember when I said that sometimes we don't struggle to hear God's voice, it's just that we don't like what He says? This would be one of those times. In Genesis 22:1–2 God called to Abraham,

> "Abraham!"
> "Here I am," he replied.
> Then God said, "Take your son, your only son, whom you love—Isaac—and go to the region of Moriah. Sacrifice him there as a burnt offering on a mountain I will show you."

1. Jennifer Kennedy Dean, *Life Unhindered* (Birmingham, AL: New Hope Publishers), 45–46.

What?! Why would God tell Abraham to take his only son (Abraham had already sent Ishmael away at God's command), the one whose name meant "laughter," the one who fulfilled all that God had promised Abraham, and sacrifice him?

Do you stop to ask these kinds of questions? I do! I especially do now that I have lived long enough to suffer the unimaginable in my life. Sometimes life's circumstances and God's goodness don't seem to line up. God confuses me. He confuses me today, and He confuses me in this story. So I look again at Genesis 22:1–2, I read it over and over, and I ask, "Lord, why did you do that?" And this is what I find:

Some time later God tested Abraham.

v. 1

There's my answer nestled right there in the first six words of the chapter. In order to test Abraham, God told him to take his precious boy and sacrifice him in Moriah.

The next question I want to ask God is this: "Lord, did you know how much Abraham loved that boy?" I mean, my husband is a godly man. To his ability he tries his best to live a life that is pleasing to God. But if God were to tell him to take his son on a trip and sacrifice him when he got there, I'm afraid that Tom would dig in his heels and say, "That ain't happenin'." Tom would give his own life for his son (or his daughters), but don't even think about asking him to give his son's life for anyone, not even God.

So I read Genesis 22:2 again and discovered that God was fully aware of the love that Abraham had for Isaac:

Take your son, your only son, whom you love—Isaac—and go . . .

God has a father's heart; He understands a father's love. Knowing this about God ought to give us a better understanding of what He endured when He watched His only Son, the One that He loved, die on the cross.

And the story continues. I'm somewhat amazed at the speed with which Abraham obeyed this word from God. If I had been him, I would have rationalized that if God took decades to fulfill His promise to me, I could maybe put off taking Isaac to Moriah for a little while. Maybe next year when he was a bit older, or when he turned sixteen and I didn't like him that much anyway. But no! Abraham got up *early* the next morning and saddled his donkey (Genesis 22:3).

According to Genesis 22:4, it took Abraham, his servants, and Isaac three days to get to Moriah. Can you even begin to imagine what those days and nights might have been like for Abraham? I picture the little band of travelers sitting around the fire at night telling stories and teasing one another. As they bantered back and forth, Abraham was unusually quiet—every once in a while a tear trickled down his face as he glanced over at his boy. But then, after everyone else was sleeping, Abraham no doubt looked into the night sky and counted the stars. When he got to 6,743, his eyelids grew heavy and he drifted off to a restless sleep, remembering the promise God made to him the first time He showed Abraham His stars.

Perhaps early in the morning Abraham rose before the others and stood over Isaac and watched him sleep. He ran his fingers through Isaac's hair and gently touched his cheekbones, savoring the smoothness of his still-boyish face. Abraham quietly considered his very own flesh and blood—proof that God keeps His promises—and gently shook his son awake.

When they arrived at Moriah, Abraham said a very interesting thing to his servants. I almost missed this the first time I read it, but after reading this story over again I almost gasped aloud. This is how Abraham did this!

> On the third day Abraham looked up and saw the place in the distance. He said to his servants, "Stay here with the donkey while I and the boy go over there. *We* will worship and then *we* will come back to you."
>
> Genesis 22:5

Notice that Abraham said *we* will worship and then *we* will come back to you. I honestly think that Abraham believed God would resurrect his son from the dead. This child was a child of promise. He was miraculously conceived and miraculously born. He was a promise for most of Abraham's life, and now he existed in the flesh—in the present. God would not . . . God could not break His promise with Abraham; therefore, God was able to do again what He had already done—the impossible in Abraham's life.

While Isaac carried the wood on his own back, Abraham carried the fire and the knife. As Isaac and Abraham hiked up the mountain, Isaac asked his dad, "I see the fire and the wood, but Dad, where's the lamb for the burnt offering?" Abraham answered, "God himself will provide the lamb, my son."

Did Abraham's heart skip a beat when he said that? Did his throat close up? It's one thing to trust God from a distance, but to be right on top of the terrible thing and know that on the other side it will all be well—in the middle of the mess it's . . . well, it's a mess! I can't help but think that Abraham might have coughed just a bit when he answered Isaac's curiosity.

When they reached the place where God told Abraham to sacrifice Isaac, Abraham built the altar, arranged the wood on it—Isaac probably helped him—and then he did the unthinkable. He seized his son firmly, bound him, and laid him on the altar. That's all the Bible tells us. Did Isaac try to get away? Did he scream for help? Did he look at his dad as if he were crazy and try to reason with him? We don't know. All we know is that Isaac didn't just hop up on top of that altar and sit still. His father bound him and placed him there.

Just as "the father of a multitude" lifted his own hand to slay "he laughs," the angel of the Lord called out, "Abraham! Stop!"

Big music in the background, flashes of scenes from all that Abraham and God have been through together, clips of Isaac as a newborn, a toddler, and little boy . . . can't you see it?

And then the angel said, "Now I know that you fear God, because you have not withheld from me your son, your only son." (I have somewhat paraphrased this story, but you can read the whole thing for yourself in Genesis 22:1–13.)

Here is the take-away for us: When God tests us, He wants to know if we believe Him. He wants to know if we are willing to die to our own reasoning, our own desires, our own needs, even our ownership of the fulfillment of His promise in our lives. Sometimes the unimaginable happens in our lives and God watches us closely to see if we are able to trust Him.

Romans 4:18–22

Abraham's faith is mentioned twice in the New Testament. Both times the New Testament writers point to him as a man who made a conscious decision to trust God.

Paul wrote this about Abraham to the church in Rome:

> *Against all hope, Abraham in hope believed* and so became the father of many nations, just as it had been said to him, "So shall your offspring be." Without weakening in his faith, *he faced the fact that his body was as good as dead.... Yet he did not waver through unbelief regarding the promise of God,* but was strengthened in his faith and gave glory to God, *being fully persuaded that God had power to do what he had promised.* This is why "it was credited to him as righteousness."
>
> Romans 4:18–22

I have several favorite parts of these verses; I've underlined them in my Bible. But my absolute favorite is the part that says, "being fully persuaded that God had power to do what he had promised." Abraham is the father of our faith because he walked with God through thick and thin and grew to recognize that "God had power to do what he had promised."

Hebrews 11:17–19

I like what the writer of Hebrews said too:

> By faith Abraham, when God tested him, offered Isaac as a sacrifice. He who had embraced the promises was about to sacrifice his one and only son, even though God had said to him, "It is through Isaac that your offspring will be reckoned." Abraham reasoned that God could even raise the dead, and so in a manner of speaking he did receive Isaac back from death.
>
> Hebrews 11:17–19

My favorite part of these verses in Hebrews is this: "Abraham reasoned that God could raise the dead, and figuratively speaking, he did receive Isaac back from the dead."

My daughter Kaleigh is an extremely logical thinker. Through the years I've discovered that it's hard for logical people to take the leap of faith. For faith often requires imagination, and logical people are not well endowed with lots of imagination. But Kaleigh chooses to believe—and during the year when our family was suffering so much trouble, Kaleigh wanted to pray as a believer. She read her Bible and I read mine, and we shared with each other the promises God gave us regarding our family's future. Some of these promises are listed for you in appendix 1.

But the realities in which we were living, and the logical conclusions of those realities, often clamored loudly to be taken into account. I have a friend who often says, "It is what it is." And while I kind of like that phrase because it often sums up the circumstances of life and reminds me that there's not a whole lot I can do to change them, it also wars against my faith. I posted this on Facebook one day: "It is what it is . . . or is it?" And I got these responses: "Hmm, for my part, it is never what it is. I have to constantly remind myself that God has a much different perspective on things, and the way things seem to be at the moment, aren't really what they seem at all!" (This quote came from my sister Amy—isn't she smart?!) And then another thought: "I really don't like the statement 'It is what it is . . . ' That's totally not true! It is what God wills it to be! That's how I view any situation where that statement comes out." (This comment is from Pinkey, a high school friend.) I love those comments; they are good reminders that God supersedes logic.

But back to my daughter whom God gifted with a logical mind. When Kaleigh was dealing with some of the heckling that goes on when you are living in between the promise and the fulfillment of the promise (the *mean* time, where Abraham lived for YEARS!), she found this verse in Hebrews. The fact that Abraham "reasoned" in his mind meant to Kaleigh that Abraham logically came to the conclusion that it would be easier for God to raise Isaac from the dead than it would be for Him to break His promise. And Kaleigh reasoned in her mind that that was true.

In the *Mean* Time Press in to God

My friends, Abraham took his precious son, Isaac, on a three-day journey, loaded his young back with wood, then bound him to the altar and raised the knife to kill his very own beloved son because Abraham BELIEVED GOD! Abraham allowed the *mean* time— the weeks, months, and years of living with reality shouting at his faith—to grow his knowledge and experiential understanding of God. As Abraham suffered the longing that came with living on the unfulfilled side of his destiny, he grew in his relationship with God. Rather than turn his back on God, he turned his face toward God. Rather than "curse God and die" (as Job's wife urged him to do), Abraham pressed in to God and refused to let go.

This is why "it was credited to him as righteousness."

Romans 4:22

If your picture doesn't match your promise—and if your promise is no longer believable—invest your grief and your longing, and your hope and your confidence in the PERSON of God.

Treasure Hunt

Personal Reflections

- I read this question in Michael Hyatt's blog: "Is Romans 8:28 still in the Bible?"[2] And the answer is: Well, yes . . . yes, it is! And since it is, I'm going to bet my boots on it—and wrap my heart around it and trust that God will hold himself to it.

  And we know that in all things God works for the good of those who love him, who have been called according to his purpose.

- Max Lucado reminds us, "It all works out in the end. If it hasn't worked out yet, then it's not the end."[3] And in Ecclesiastes 7:8 we read,

  The end of a matter is better than its beginning, and patience is better than pride.

Discussion Questions

1. Take a few minutes to reflect on the many promises God has already kept for you. Share one of these with your group.
2. Consider the most precious person in your life. Do you allow your love for him or her to supersede your love for God?

---

2. Michael Hyatt, "Is Romans 8:28 still in the Bible?" Intentional Leadership, posted February 23, 2011, http://michaelhyatt.com/is-romans-8-28-still-in-the-bible.html.
3. Ibid.

3. What is happening in your life that causes you to doubt God? How might you "reason in your mind" that God will come through for you in that situation?

Treasure Verse

Yet he did not waver through unbelief regarding the promise of God, but was strengthened in his faith and gave glory to God, being fully persuaded that God had power to do what he had promised.

Romans 4:20–21

PART TWO

Where Was
God When . . . ?

In the next few chapters you will discover the answer to "Where was God when . . . ?" So many times we allow the circumstances of our lives to define God's goodness. Sometimes we let life's circumstances squeeze themselves in between our hearts and God. When we do this, life's "stuff" casts shadows on God's glory. It's hard to hear God's voice in the shadow land. Walk with me now through the stories of Joseph, Hezekiah, and Jesus' disciples to learn how to posture yourself so that life's "stuff" can't get between you and God.

> If we come to see the purpose of the universe as God's long-term glory rather than our short-term happiness, then we will undergo a critical paradigm shift in tackling the problem of evil and suffering.
>
> —Randy Alcorn [1]

---

1. Randy Alcorn, *Ninety Days of God's Goodness* (Colorado Springs: Multnomah, 2011), 35, www.reviveourhearts.com/articles/selected-quotes-90-days -gods-goodness/.

7

Where Was God When Joseph Was in the Pit?

"For I know the plans I have for you," declares the Lord, "plans to prosper you and not to harm you, plans to give you hope and a future."

Jeremiah 29:11

Thus far in this book you have walked with Jacob (Israel) and Abraham through their very real journeys of faith. I hope that you've come to appreciate the privilege we have to take hold of the Person of God and refuse to let go until He accomplishes all that He's promised. In my quest to teach you how to hear the voice of God, I want you to recognize His invitations to wrestle. Be sure to remember that the *mean* time—that period of time that exists between God's promise and His fulfillment of it—is the *main* time for you to grow in your faith.

As your faith grows, so will your ability to hear the voice of God. As your ability to hear the voice of God grows, so will your ministry. God uses those who develop ears to hear His voice. God longs to demonstrate His power and His love through the lives of His children. As you grow in your ability to hear the voice of God, don't be surprised if God chooses to use your life to demonstrate His glory. Read on and discover how He did this with Joseph.

Leading to the Pit

Joseph's story is found in Genesis 37, 39–50. As always, I tend to embellish the retelling of these stories, so I encourage you to take the time to read it word for word in your copy of the Bible. But since this is my book, I get to tell my version.

Joseph was seventeen when we first met him and discovered that he was his father's favorite. We're told that Joseph was favored by his father, Jacob, because he was born to him in his old age. Now, I would have never understood this had I not just become a "Nana" in my "old age." (Not that forty-seven is old for a Nana, but I can only imagine the spoiling I might do to a child of my own at this stage of my life!) When Misty (my granddaughter) was about six months old, Mikel and I enjoyed taking her shopping. One of our favorite outings was to Target, where we could find an assortment of age-appropriate toys. In my book, playing is Misty's job, and I want her to be well-equipped to do a good job. On one of our Target outings, every toy Mikel and I showed Misty resulted in this reaction: First she flexed her arms and legs, then she curled her toes. After that, her entire body shook with delight as documented by a great big smile on her gorgeous face. It was as if we'd just shown her the *very thing* that gave her the absolute most joy in the whole wide world!

Now, a year later at eighteen months of age, Misty simply brings whatever her heart desires to me and I put it in the cart! (When she shops with her mother, she pulls her chosen treasure off the shelf and makes a beeline for the door.) Honey, if I'd had my own children at the age I am now, they'd be even more rotten than they already are. That baby will have whatever she wants if I have anything to do with it!

But I digress. Joseph was not only his father's favorite, but he was also a tattletale. He was the one who always ran back and yelled, "Daddy, did you know that Dan and Gad were smoking behind the bushes?"

There are several coats mentioned in Scripture, and Joseph was wearing one of them. His dad gave it to him because he loved him, and his brothers hated him for it. Genesis 37:4 says,

> When his brothers saw that their father loved him more than any of them, they hated him and could not speak a kind word to him.

So Joseph never was a part of the brotherhood. Brothers can be terribly cruel—but even if they do make you fall flat on your face when you leap from a tree in complete confidence that they will be just below to catch you (something that Tom's brother did to him)—when push comes to shove, they will almost always stand up for you. My husband, Tom, is the youngest of four boys, and he can attest to this ancient truth. But that was not the case with Joseph's brothers. They hated him. To make matters worse, Joseph had some dreams. And although God gave him some incredible dreams, God didn't give Joseph the good sense to keep those dreams to himself:

> Hey guys, listen to the dream I just had. We were harvesting the grain out in the fields when suddenly, my sheaf of grain rose and stood upright while all ya'll's gathered around and bowed down! (Genesis 37:5–7, paraphrase)

When Joseph shared his dream, his brothers hated him all the more! Can't you just imagine the merciless teasing Joseph got as a result of sharing his dream? Then he had another dream. Don't share it, Joseph! Not a good idea! But no . . . Joseph, all excited about the possibilities of a glorious future, decided to share his enthusiasm with his brothers: "You're not gonna believe this, but I had another dream . . ."

"I think I'm feeling sick," one brother said to another.

". . . only this time the sun and moon and eleven stars were bowing down to me."

Even Joseph's father rebuked him for this dream. "Are you saying that your mother and I *and* your eleven brothers are *all* going to bow down to you?!"

Genesis 37:11 tells us that while Joseph's brothers were eaten up with jealousy, his father "kept the matter in mind." Now, I don't know about you, but as a parent there are some matters that happen in my children's lives that I "keep in mind." My son is finishing up a summer of campaigning for a Tennessee state house congressional candidate. Over the past eight weeks, TJ has knocked on most every door in the Thompson Station/Spring Hill community. Hardly a day goes by when I don't receive an email or a Facebook message from a church member or community friend bragging on my son. I'm "keeping this in mind." When TJ was a toddler, we took him out for ice cream. While we waited on Dad to get our treats to the table, TJ went visiting the others enjoying their ice cream in the parlor. He walked from table to table saying this: "Hi, I'm TJ, what's your name?" One customer exclaimed, "He's either going to be a preacher or a politician when he grows up." I've "kept that in mind."

So Joseph shared his dreams and Jacob "kept them in mind." Dreams or no dreams, as happens in many families to this day, the undercurrent of jealousy, frustration, and ill will culminated one day when Joseph was sent by his father to go check on the others. Unlike the day that David's father sent him to check on *his* brothers, Joseph was NOT about to take a giant down. No . . . the giant of jealousy was about to toss Joseph in a pit. And to the human eye, Joseph's life was about to take a tailspin as far away from God's promises (as hinted at in Joseph's dreams) as he could possibly be.

But let me remind you here that just as with David, God was meticulously and methodically working His plans and His purposes in Joseph's life.

Isaiah 55:8–11 says this,

"For my thoughts are not your thoughts, neither are your ways my ways," declares the Lord. *"As the heavens are higher than the earth, so are my ways higher than yours and my thoughts than your thoughts.* As the rain and the snow come down from heaven, and do not return to it without watering the earth and making it bud and flourish, so that it yields seed for the sower and bread for the eater, *so is my word that goes out from my mouth: It will not return to me empty, but will accomplish what I desire and achieve the purpose for which I sent it."*

Here is the first answer to our question: Where was God when Joseph was in the pit? Right there with him! Only God was thinking higher thoughts, managing higher ways, and making certain that the "word" that came to Joseph in the form of a couple crazy dreams would indeed achieve the purpose He intended for it to achieve.

Where is God in your pit? He's in there with you—thinking higher thoughts and navigating better ways. He is even now making sure that the promises He's made to you will achieve His purposes.

In the Pit

Poor Joseph. I know that he knew his brothers hated him— he had to know! But most likely, being the golden child of the tribe, he refused to entertain the possibility that anything could separate him from the privileged life of favor that he'd grown to appreciate.

I can relate to Joseph. Before 2010 I actually had people tell me that my life was a fairy tale. They told me that I lived the life others dreamed of and that I couldn't possibly relate to them and their troubles because I'd never had very many of my own. And they were mostly right. Up until 2010 I had very few troubles at all.

I am of the mind now that because of that fairy tale, the pits are even nastier. Children who wear decorated robes are not accustomed to mud, centipedes, and salamanders. They have no training for life when it isn't served up on a silver platter. Beautifully ornamented coats are *not* designed for slavery! Joseph was no doubt bewildered, undone, and devastated by the cruel reality of life when he bumped his bum on the wet bottom of that pit.

It was Reuben's idea to put him there. Although we see it as Joseph's worst possible scenario, it was much better than being dead—and had Reuben not suggested the pit, his brothers surely would have killed him. But Reuben must've had to go to the bathroom or find a lost sheep or do something that took him away from his brothers. For when the Ishmaelites came along, Judah suggested they turn their brother into profit and sell him rather than kill him. So Joseph was sold to the Ishmaelites for twenty pieces of silver.

Let's pause here for a moment and recognize the irony of Joseph being sold to the Ishmaelites. The Ishmaelites were actually distant relatives of Joseph and his brothers. Their forefather was Abraham! Only the Ishmaelites were descended from Ishmael—Sarah's failed attempt to help God keep his promise to her husband. Don't you find it a bit ironic? It was as if some power of darkness—let's just come right out and call him Satan—were rubbing salt in an old wound!

The Ishmaelites were not a part of the promise of God. Spiritual battles are being fought all the time. And because Joseph had already shared his dreams of how God was going to do great and mighty things in his life, the devil was on to him. I think that the devil wanted to take Joseph out—to wipe away his faith and strip away his dreams. So while any kind of foreigner might have traveled through Dothan that evening, it was the Ishmaelites . . . the not-a-part-of-the-promise people!

Do you feel as if your dreams have been sold to the imposter . . . the not-a-part-of-the-promise of God? Were you living your life headed toward the fulfillment of your dreams only to be thrown into a slimy pit, then sold to the "not God's plan," and driven full speed in the opposite direction? Are your hopes being driven to Egypt by Ishmaelites? *Not Egypt! That is in the opposite direction of all that God has promised me!* Canaan was Joseph's Promised Land! Not Egypt!

Where was God when Joseph was sold into slavery? He was nodding His head and whispering in his disillusioned ears,

> For I know the plans I have for you . . . plans to prosper you and not to harm you, plans to give you hope and a future. Then you will call on me and come and pray to me, and I will listen to you. You will seek me and find me when you seek me with all your heart. I will be found by you . . . and will bring you back from captivity. I will gather you from all the nations and places where I have banished you . . . and will bring you back to the place from which I carried you into exile.
>
> Jeremiah 29:11–14

Take a minute to consider what God was doing:

- God was making sure that Reuben had enough conscience to suggest putting Joseph in a pit when his brothers were raging for blood!
- God was appealing to Judah's greed when the Ishmaelites "just happened" to be traveling smack-dab through Dothan so that Joseph would be sold into slavery and make his way to Egypt.
- Joseph might have thought that God had gone somewhere else that day, but God was meticulously and methodically seeing to it that even what the devil meant for harm would be transformed to good.

Where is God on your journey into exile? He is whispering in your ear, "I know the plans I have for you . . . plans to prosper you and not to harm you, plans to give you a hope and a future."

We have the advantage of knowing what's coming next in Joseph's story, but when Joseph was taken to Egypt, he didn't know. If we could sit nearby and hear him that night when the Ishmaelites were asleep, this is what we might hear him say: "Oh God! I miss my dad! How could my brothers have done such a thing? What kind of evil does this? You promised me! What about the bowing sheaves and stars? This is *not* a good idea! These plans don't prosper me!"

I don't know that Joseph did that, but I did it! I spent weeks and months arguing with God that the pit, those blasted Ishmaelites, and then Egypt were *not* in keeping with the plans that were promised me in Jeremiah 29:11.

But thankfully this was not the end of Joseph's story, and if you find yourself in this place, it's not the end of yours either.

Learning to Live in Egypt

Joseph's journey continued. . . . After taking him to Egypt, the Ishmaelites sold Joseph to Potiphar, one of Pharaoh's officials, the captain of the guard. This is where Joseph begins to teach us a valuable lesson. If we continue with our question, "Where was God when Joseph was sold to Potiphar?" then Genesis 39:2 answers that question:

> *The Lord was with Joseph so that he prospered,* and he lived in the house of his Egyptian master.

By the time Joseph arrived in Potiphar's service, he determined to live in the present moment. While he could have slipped into depression and spent his waking hours wondering what his family was doing, the Scripture tells us that he succeeded in everything he did as he served in Potiphar's home (Genesis 39:2). Joseph could not have been such a success had he spent his time grieving the past and dreaming of the future. I learned that the abundant life is experienced in the *present* . . . not in the past . . . and not in the future, but in the present.

This is the day the Lord has made; we will rejoice and be glad in it!

Psalm 118:24 NKJV

If we keep our minds in the past we let regret, remorse, grief, and shame consume the blessings God pours on us today. Don't do that! If we let our minds spill over into the future, we are bombarded with anxiety, fear, and dread over what we imagine might happen there, and again we miss the presence—and the power—of God in our today. Don't do that!

Jesus said, "I have come that they may have life, and have it to the full" (John 10:10).

That life is today!

I cannot begin to tell you how powerful this discipline of living in the present moment is. For Joseph, it not only blessed him, but it also blessed the ones who were in the present moment with him. Potiphar's entire house was blessed along with Joseph.

I struggle with keeping my mind set on the present. My thoughts tend to wander to yesterday and make endless lists of regrets. Not only do I look behind me, but I also look ahead. I have a vast imagination and I love to script the future. But when I do that, I miss the abundance of life that God has given me today. In fact, the only life I really live, I live right now.

One of the best ways to develop the ability to hear God's voice is to commit to the discipline of a quiet time. For a few minutes every morning I read from the Bible and pray. Often I "hear" God speak to me through His Word, or I sense Him putting thoughts into my mind and heart with truth based on what I read in His Word. God gave me this truth one morning when I was praying for my children: *If we truly believe that God is intimately acquainted with our deepest desires and that His sovereignty rules the details of our lives, we will rest in our current circumstances no matter what they are.*

101

I believe that Joseph embraced this truth. While he had plenty of reasons to think that God had abandoned him to slavery (and later to prison), his behavior proves that he didn't waste mental and emotional energy fighting that battle. When Joseph was in Potiphar's house, he served so faithfully that Potiphar put him in charge of his entire household and everything he owned (Genesis 39:5). Then, when Joseph was in prison, he won the favor of the prison warden and was also put in charge there. Had Joseph spent his time worrying over what happened *to* him in the past, had he harbored bitterness toward his brothers, had he wasted energy grieving what was bound to happen in his future, he would not have been successful in his present circumstances.

Joseph's reward for keeping his heart and mind focused on God's intimate involvement in his life resulted in a gift far better than any other. Joseph experienced God granting him favor on a daily basis. Even when Mrs. Potiphar tried to seduce him, and Joseph was wrongly accused of attempted rape and then thrown into prison,

> . . . *the Lord was with him*; he showed him kindness and granted him favor in the eyes of the prison warden.
>
> Genesis 39:21

My friend, Joseph couldn't do anything about his jealous brothers. He couldn't change them, he couldn't talk them out of their evil schemes, nor could he gain a thing by wondering how they could have been so different having been raised in the same home. Joseph could not win when accused of assaulting Potiphar's wife. I would imagine that even Potiphar knew the truth, but what was he to do? Favor a slave over his own wife? But Joseph could accept the fact that God was intimately acquainted with his deepest desires and that God's sovereignty ruled the details of his life. Therefore, even in the dungeons of Egypt, Joseph could rest (and prosper).

I love this story of Joseph. For although he was chosen by God for greatness, he was mistreated, slandered, and cheated.

But rather than waste his energy trying to change others, or spinning his wheels whining over God's apparent neglect, Joseph instead chose to trust God. And when Joseph accepted the fact that life simply "is what it is" (or perhaps life is what God allows it to be), he found rest in his current circumstances. While there are no verses that actually tell us that "Joseph found rest," we do read several that tell us he "succeeded in everything he did" (Genesis 39:2), that the Lord "gave him success" (Genesis 39:3), and that his success was rewarded with promotion (Genesis 39:4 and 39:22). We are also told that God "showed [Joseph] his faithful love" and made him a favorite (Genesis 39:21). From these verses I surmise that Joseph found rest as he made the choice to live his life trusting his past and future to God while he served God in his present.

When we learn the secret of truly believing that God is intimately acquainted with our deepest desires and that His sovereignty rules the details of our lives, we will rest in our current circumstances:

- whether we are sleeping in our father's house wrapped in a beautiful robe,
- enjoying the wealth and privilege of Egypt's prosperous citizens,
- or lying on the cold, hard floor of a damp dungeon.

Where was God when Joseph was in that prison? He was *right there with him.* Not only meticulously and methodically working out the plans He'd made long before Joseph was ever born, but also preparing Joseph to assume a very important role in Egypt.

God may have you in your prison today because that prison is the only place you will learn the skills, compassion, and incredible truths that will sustain you when He elevates you to a position of authority in your future. Don't waste your prison time pining over what shoulda, woulda, coulda been. Don't exhaust your energy painting pictures of what might be. Simply live in the present moment and anticipate the abundance of God's promises as He appropriates them to you in this moment.

Expect God to be there, in that prison with you, fulfilling His Word in your life:

> And my God will meet all your needs according to the riches of his glory in Christ Jesus.
>
> Philippians 4:19

God Always Does What He Says He Will Do

You may already know the rest of the story . . . the baker and the taster were thrown into prison with Joseph and they both had dreams. They woke up and were eager to figure out what their dreams meant. The taster shared his first, and Joseph told him that his prison visit was soon to come to an end. The baker was encouraged by the taster's dream, and so he shared his dream too. Unfortunately for the baker, his interpretation was not as favorable as that of the taster, and three days later the baker died and the taster resumed his service to Pharaoh. (Just as Joseph had predicted.)

Although Joseph had asked the taster to speak to Pharaoh on his behalf, the taster forgot all about him. Joseph's hopes were dashed, and he entered a season of silence and waiting. This is perhaps worse than the pit. The pit is terrible—there's no doubt about that—but the silence and monotony of living day in and day out without a glimmer of hope reassuring you that God is *on it* might even be worse. For two years Joseph lived those kinds of days.

But eventually Pharaoh had a dream too. Long story short, the taster suddenly remembered the man who was a great interpreter of dreams, and Joseph came out of his cell. And Pharaoh made Joseph second only to himself. Joseph lived the life of favor he was destined to live, and eventually his own family bowed down to him *just like Joseph's dreams said they would many years before.*

So what does all this mean to you today?

- Even if you are in a pit . . .
- Even if the Ishmaelites (not a part of God's promise) are taking you far from the place you *know* God means for you to be . . .
- Even if Mrs. Potiphar has accused you of wrongdoing and you are living in a dungeon forgotten by the one person who has the ability to get you out . . .

No matter where you are—no matter what is going on—God is meticulously and methodically proving himself faithful to you.

But don't miss this final truth. All this—Joseph's dream and his entire journey—were not about Joseph at all. This entire plan was designed in the heart of God to save the people of Israel from the famine so that God could keep a promise He'd made to Abraham a long time ago. Why? Because God *always* keeps His promises! What God is doing in your life is not just about you. Today He is not only making sure that He keeps every promise He has ever made to you, but He is also still keeping the promises He made to Abraham. And what exactly was that promise?

Genesis 12:2 says, "I will bless you and you will be a blessing" (my paraphrase).

God is blessing you even now in your pit. And you will be a blessing. As you allow God to complete the good work He began in you, you will be a blessing to others.

I had coffee with a friend this past summer. She has had many more pits in her life than I have had in mine. So when she said what I'm about to share with you, she was completely qualified to share it. This is what she told me: "Leighann, you've got to stop complaining about the absurdity of your situation and instead allow God to use you in it. This has become your platform. Use it to bring Him glory."

I know that your platform was probably not of your choosing. Who would possibly want to experience what you have experienced? Perhaps you are still being led toward Egypt by your Ishmaelites.

But when you get there, and when you are able to come to a place where you know you know you know . . .

. . . that God is right there beside you in your pit—bringing His higher thoughts and ways . . .

. . . that He still knows the plans He has for your life—that they are for your good (and not to harm you) . . .

And when you know you know you know that the life you live today can be full of not only God's provision but also His abundance, then the time will come when you can say with Joseph,

> . . . but God intended [this pit] for good. [He had in mind all along] to accomplish what is now being done, the saving of many lives.
>
> Genesis 50:20

Treasure Hunt

Personal Reflection

- Read Joseph's story in Genesis 37, 39–50.
- Consider your own life. If you were living in Joseph's story, where might you be today? In the pit? On the way to Egypt? In Potiphar's house? Falsely accused? In the dungeon? Or ruling Egypt?
- What do you need to do to embrace this statement?

    If we truly believe that God is intimately acquainted with our deepest desires and that His sovereignty rules the details of our lives, we will rest in our current circumstances no matter what they are.

Discussion Questions

1. What new insights did you gain from the retelling of Joseph's story?

2. Share a time when your life mirrored Joseph's. If God has brought you to the other side of that experience, share what He did.

3. Which bad day do you think was the worst for Joseph? The day his brothers tossed him in the pit? The day Potiphar's wife falsely accused him? The day after the taster went back to Pharaoh? Why do you think that one was the worst?

4. Who do you think God is impacting with your life? Are you willing to suffer for God's best for them?

Treasure Verse

"For my thoughts are not your thoughts, neither are your ways my ways," declares the Lord. *"As the heavens are higher than the earth, so are my ways higher than your ways and my thoughts than your thoughts.* As the rain and the snow come down from heaven, and do not return to it without watering the earth and making it bud and flourish, so that it yields seed for the sower and bread for the eater, *so is my word that goes out from my mouth: It will not return to me empty, but will accomplish what I desire and achieve the purpose for which I sent it."*

Isaiah 55:8–11

8

Where Was God When Hezekiah Was Being Good?

Hezekiah trusted in the Lord, the God of Israel. There was no one like him among all the kings of Judah, either before him or after him. He held fast to the Lord and did not stop following him; he kept the commands the Lord had given Moses. And the Lord was with him; he was successful in whatever he undertook.

2 Kings 18:5–7

Many times we expect God to act in accordance with our logical assumptions. For instance, we think that if we do _____ (you fill in the blank—anything good, wholesome, worthy), then we can expect God to reward us with _____ (you fill in the blank—prosperity, good health, well-grounded children who make right choices, the list can go on and on). One of the most difficult things about hearing the voice of God during seasons of disappointment and crisis is that, try as you may, you cannot logically process the circumstances you find yourself in. That's what baffles and confuses you! If the circumstances you find yourself in right now make no sense at all—meaning that there is no logical explanation for their existence—you can be sure the Enemy is on the move and God is still in control.

This chapter is going to be about how to hear the voice of God when the circumstances of your life are confusing. I'll start by sharing with you that my cancer baffles me. I think it's a direct Enemy attack. Let me explain why I think it fits in the category of an attack from the Enemy. I know that cancer is no respecter of persons, but when I read of the dietary and lifestyle habits that ought to be embraced as a guard against the disease, I have to confess that I have done those things. Also, there has been no hereditary cancer in my lineage. My father was diagnosed with prostate cancer a few years ago, but I understand that many men deal with prostate cancer when they get to a certain age. Besides, I don't have a prostate, so I figure that cancer doesn't count for me.

I read in my surgeon's office two years ago that a person like me has less than a 2 percent chance of ever contracting colon cancer. Perhaps that is why my symptoms were dismissed so readily when I asked my doctor about them for several years before we had a diagnosis. Not only that, but my cancer was diagnosed the week I received a contract for writing my book *Spiritual Warfare for Women*. After surgery I was told that I had an 89 percent chance of being cured of cancer—that it most likely would not recur. So when I began writing this book and discovered that my cancer had returned in my liver, the timing seemed to be more than coincidence.

Not every bad thing that happens to you has Satan as its author, but he is real and his attacks are inevitable, especially if you desire to live a life that demonstrates God's power. That's the bad news. The good news is that each attack of the Enemy brings with it a perfect opportunity for God to work in ways that are supernatural for your good and His glory.

Navigating Crazy

I was in Germany a few years ago in September. My dear friend and prayer partner and I were leading a prayer conference for a church that ministered to our American military personnel serving at both the Ramstein Air Force Base and Vogelweh Army Post. My friend and I had a great time together as we toured the surrounding area with our tour guide. We were quite the adventurers. With nothing more than a full tank of petrol and a GPS in our little European car, we took off completely confident in the little black box that told us which way to go.

We navigated our way through the Swiss Alps, several tiny Italian villages, and even the vineyards of France. But one night after dark, we found ourselves on cobblestone streets in a little German village that had a HUGE bridge missing in the middle of their road. For a bit we'd seen the signs warning us that the road was closed ahead, but our GPS said go—so off we went. Once we realized there was no way we would ever get around that missing bridge, we entered crazy. No matter which way we turned, that GPS wanted to send us right back to the gaping hole in the middle of that village road.

That's the way I feel when the circumstances of life catch me off guard. I have my full confidence in the Word of God and the trusted ways of God (that I've experienced through the years), but then something incredible happens to me or to someone I love, and suddenly God doesn't seem to know what He's doing. This happened to Hezekiah. Before I tell my version of Hezekiah's story, let me remind you to read it for yourself. You will find his story in 2 Kings 18–19; 2 Chronicles 32; and Isaiah 36–37.

Hezekiah was a good king—even though he'd had a bad father. Hezekiah was the grandson of Zechariah, and I'm going to assume he had a great relationship with his grandfather. For Scripture says that Hezekiah "trusted in the Lord, the God of Israel. . . . He held fast to the Lord and did not stop following him" (2 Kings 18:5–6).

Isn't that great? Even though he had a father who "did not do what was right in the eyes of the Lord" (2 Kings 16:2), Hezekiah decided to go with God. He used his position as king over Judah to ignite revival amongst the people. But right in the midst of doing a whole lot of great things for God, Hezekiah came face-to-face with a national crisis. As we visit with Hezekiah, we're going to answer this question: *Where was God when Hezekiah was being good?*

Hezekiah's Good Work

Although Hezekiah's father, King Ahaz, "made idols for worshiping the Baals," "burned sacrifices in the Valley of Ben Hinnom," and even "sacrificed his children in the fire" (2 Chronicles 28:2–3), when Hezekiah became king at twenty-five years of age, he "did what was right in the eyes of the Lord" (2 Kings 18:3). I'd love to know more about Hezekiah's childhood so that I could understand how he evaded the poor influence of his father, but Scripture doesn't tell us that story. We do, however, get to discover the kind of man that Hezekiah was by seeing the kinds of projects he completed.

In 2 Chronicles 29–31 we discover that Hezekiah did these good things:

1. "In the first month of the first year of his reign, he opened the doors of the temple of the Lord and repaired them" (2 Chronicles 29:3).
2. He brought in the priests and the Levites, assembled them, consecrated them, and put them back in their places of spiritual leadership (2 Chronicles 29:4–11).
3. He reinstated the burnt offerings and the fellowship offerings, thanksgiving and praises in the house of the Lord (2 Chronicles 29:31).
4. He gave the sacrifices to be offered for worship from his own possessions (2 Chronicles 31:3).
5. He charged the people with giving their tithes to support the priests and Levites (2 Chronicles 31:4).
6. The people gave so generously that Hezekiah gave orders to prepare storerooms in the temple to hold their offerings (2 Chronicles 31:5–11).

Scripture records Hezekiah's good works with this statement in 2 Chronicles 31:20–21:

> This is what Hezekiah did throughout Judah, doing what was good and right and faithful before the Lord his God. In everything that he undertook in the service of God's temple and in obedience to the laws and the commands, he sought his God and worked wholeheartedly.

And don't miss the next sentence—one that I am quite happy with (v. 21):

> "And so he prospered."

I like that sentence because *that* is what I expect from God when His men and women serve Him well. Prosperity follows obedience. I lived my life as a faithful testimony to this truth for many years. I was like David when he professed, "When I felt secure, I said, 'I will never be shaken.' Lord, when you favored me, you made my mountain stand firm" (Psalm 30:6–7). Many of us live for years favored by God. We are so accustomed to God's favor that we don't even know He is making our mountain stand firm. It isn't until your mountain shakes that you realize you took for granted the days and years it stood firm.

Don't you wish that Hezekiah's story could end with "and so he prospered"? Don't you wish that if we would just do what was good and right and faithful before the Lord, we could anticipate that *each* and *every* time He would in return prosper us? Isn't that what the Scripture tells us we can expect? After all, my life verse is Jeremiah 29:11:

> "For I know the plans I have for you," declares the Lord, "plans to prosper you and not to harm you, plans to give you hope and a future."

These are the plans God has for me . . . aren't they? David described my sentiments exactly as he continued in his psalm, "But when you hid your face, I was dismayed" (Psalm 30:7). Like David I thought, *I will never be shaken,* but during the past few years of my life, I have been dismayed. If you feel like David and me, you're going to enjoy Hezekiah's story.

What Is Sennacherib, King of Assyria, Doing in This Story?

But Hezekiah's story is only just beginning. And although he was found faithful and God was pleased with his obedience, his prosperity was about to be challenged.

> After all that Hezekiah had so faithfully done, Sennacherib king of Assyria came and invaded Judah. He laid siege to the fortified cities, thinking to conquer them for himself.
>
> 2 Chronicles 32:1

What is Sennacherib doing in this story? Hezekiah is supposed to be rewarded for his wholehearted faith. He should anticipate peace on every side and a nation that experiences prosperity. Obedience to God is a recipe for success . . . right?

But Sennacherib had no regard for Hezekiah's God. The Assyrian king intended to conquer Judah for himself. Sennacherib was driven by ambition, greed, and pagan appetites that are never satisfied. He was doing what pagan kings do—invading and conquering his neighbors.

Can I just say this happens to us today? There are plenty of pagan "kings" who have appetites that are never satisfied. They do what pagan kings do—invade and attempt to conquer God's children. Consider cancer, pornography, adultery, poverty, natural disasters . . . and the list could go on and on.

The first thing Hezekiah did when he saw that Sennacherib intended to attack Jerusalem was respond with military wisdom. After consulting his officials and military staff, he blocked off the water from the springs outside the city—meaning he shut off the city's water source so that Sennacherib's army couldn't invade the city through the aquaducts. Then Hezekiah repaired and reinforced the city wall. He also made more weapons and shields. After this he set up marshal law and assembled everyone before him so that he could make this speech:

> "Be strong and courageous. Do not be afraid or discouraged because of the king of Assyria and the vast army with him, for there is a greater power with us than with him. With him is only the arm of flesh, but with us is the Lord our God to help us and to fight our battles." And the people gained confidence from what Hezekiah the king of Judah said.
>
> 2 Chronicles 32:7–8

I wouldn't expect anything but this from a man like Hezekiah. He was most definitely a man of wisdom, faith, and conviction. But even after he made preparations on the home front and professed confidence in the Lord his God, Hezekiah's situation grew worse. Sennacherib laid siege to Lachish, then sent his officers to Jerusalem with a message for Hezekiah and all his people. Sennacherib challenged the citizens of Jerusalem by challenging Hezekiah's confidence that God would save them. He told them that Hezekiah was misleading them and that he (Sennacherib) had already destroyed the people of other lands—their gods had done nothing to save them. He went on to say:

> Do not let Hezekiah deceive you and mislead you like this. Do not believe him, for no god of any nation or kingdom has been able to deliver his people from my hand or the hand of my predecessors. How much less will your god deliver you from my hand!
>
> 2 Chronicles 32:15

Sennacherib's officers said a lot more; Sennacherib even wrote letters insulting God and Hezekiah. This entourage of Assyrian officers even spoke in the Hebrew language so that the people understood what they said. You can read this in 2 Chronicles 32:9–19.

Oh my goodness! Has this ever happened to you? You believe, you profess, you live your faith out loud—but the devil just keeps tearing away at it. He heckles you; he challenges your childlike faith just like Sennacherib heckled Hezekiah and the citizens of Jerusalem. Here's how this is happening to me as I write these words.

"On what are you basing your confidence?" the devil hollered from the other side of the surgeon who just removed half my liver and told me there was a 65 percent chance the tumors would return again.

"Uhhh, on the promise God gave me that He will come through for me!" I timidly responded.

"Why are you clinging to your worthless faith? Why not just give in and go with the flow? Why not give up and accept things as they are?" He continued to yell as I looked up my particular cancer and read the stats on those who survive past five years.

"Because I want to believe that 'the Lord our God will help me fight this battle!'" I am beginning to get a bit of fight back in my heart and my remaining half a liver!

"Do you not know what I have done to the others who've found themselves in your position?" he heckled on.

"Yes! Yes I do! Only 8 or 10 percent made it past five years, if I understand the statistics right. . . ."

That's how my most recent confrontation went. This could apply to your crisis too. Is it your marriage? Rarely ever do marriages experience the miracles of reconciliation. Is it your children? Perhaps the devil is telling you that the decisions they made several years ago have destined them for lifetimes of regret. Maybe it's your church. Oh, how the devil likes to keep God's churches in his wicked clutches. What else?

Sennacherib told the citizens of Jerusalem that no other god had proved stronger than him, and their god would be no different from the others. Is your Enemy telling you the same thing? My friend, when you are dealing with crises in your life, you cannot look around and predict your outcome. God said,

> Forget the former things; do not dwell on the past. See, I am doing a new thing! Now it springs up; do you not perceive it? I am making a way in the wilderness and streams in the wasteland.
>
> Isaiah 43:18–19

God is doing a *new thing*! What happened then ain't happening now! He is up to something better . . . bigger and bolder! When Sennacherib's officers camp out on the outskirts of your town and begin to heckle you—"Be strong and courageous. Do not be afraid or discouraged . . . for there is a greater power with us than with him!" (2 Chronicles 32:7).

Say that aloud with me now: "There is a greater power with us than with him!"

The Enemy's Intent

For days Sennacherib camped his army in the shadow of Jerusalem and called out in Hebrew to the people huddled thirsty on the other side of the recently fortified wall. Those officers had one goal in mind: "to terrify them and make them afraid in order to capture the city" (2 Chronicles 32:18). Several times in Scripture this is the tactic the Enemy takes. Remember Goliath? He shouted his defiance, and Israel's soldiers ran in fear (1 Samuel 17).

I met the chief of police in Spring Hill, Tennessee, on the tenth anniversary of 9/11. Our church joined with the other churches in our community to host a prayer meeting at the city hall on that Sunday afternoon. I expressed how grateful I was that we seem to be winning this war on terror. He solemnly told me that so far the day had been a good day. But he believed there would be another attack—it was just a matter of time. He then went on to say that most people believe the next one will come to a small community in order to instill widespread fear in Americans who live in small communities across our nation—knowing that anything could happen anywhere.

I'm thankful for law enforcement officers who are diligent to protect us. But I refuse to live my life in fear that is generated by an Enemy who has nothing but threats. Sure—he can give you cancer, even one that metastasizes—but God holds your life in His hands. He can mess with your marriage—but God is the One who can transform whatever the Enemy meant to harm you and use *that very thing* to create a greater bond between you. That Enemy can also deceive and hijack your children, but God is the One who delights over them and will bring them home wiser, stronger, more than what they ever could have been without the Enemy's attack.

The Enemy has the ability to do only what God gives him permission to do. The only power he has over you is the power you give him when you allow his words and empty threats to make you afraid. When you start to fear, try reciting 2 Chronicles 32:7–8, inserting your own circumstances:

> Be strong and courageous. Do not be afraid or discouraged because of _____ (you fill in the blank). For there is a greater power with us than with him. With him is only the arm of flesh, but with us is the Lord our God to help us and to fight our battles.

The Lord Will Fight Our Battles

When Hezekiah heard Sennacherib's officers, he "cried out in prayer" with the prophet Isaiah. Here is a good word for you. When you are battling the Enemy—find a prayer partner. Connect with someone whose faith is strong and pray together! Hezekiah connected with the prophet Isaiah. Turn in your Bibles to Isaiah 37 so that you can get the entire story.

> When King Hezekiah heard this, he tore his clothes and put on sackcloth and went into the temple of the Lord. He sent Eliakim the

palace administrator, Shebna the secretary, and the leading priests, all wearing sackcloth, to the prophet Isaiah son of Amoz. They told him, "This is what Hezekiah says: This day is a day of distress and rebuke and disgrace, as when children come to the moment of birth and there is no strength to deliver them. It may be that the Lord your God will hear the words of the field commander, whom his master, the king of Assyria, has sent to ridicule the living God, and that he will rebuke him for the words the Lord your God has heard. Therefore pray for the remnant that still survives."

Isaiah 37:1–4

Upon hearing this report, Isaiah said this:

Tell your master, "This is what the Lord says: Do not be afraid of what you have heard—those words with which the underlings of the king of Assyria have blasphemed me. Listen! When he hears a certain report, I will make him want to return to his own country, and there I will have him cut down with the sword."

Isaiah 37:5–7

But what I really love is Hezekiah's prayer recorded in verses 14–20.

Hezekiah received the letter from the messengers and read it. Then he went up to the temple of the Lord and spread it out before the Lord. And Hezekiah prayed to the Lord: "Lord Almighty, the God of Israel, enthroned between the cherubim, you alone are God over all the kingdoms of the earth. You have made heaven and earth. Give ear, Lord, and hear; open your eyes, Lord, and see; listen to all the words Sennacherib has sent to ridicule the living God.

"It is true, Lord, that the Assyrian kings have laid waste all these peoples and their lands. They have thrown their gods into the fire and destroyed them, for they were not gods but only wood and stone, fashioned by human hands. Now, Lord our God, deliver us from his hand, so that all the kingdoms of the earth may know that you, Lord, are the only God."

Isaiah 37:14–20

And after Hezekiah prayed, Isaiah delivered God's response. Read it in Isaiah 37:21–35. Basically Isaiah told Hezekiah that "because you have prayed" (verse 21), God is going to show up! God delivered His word very specifically and meant every word He said. The part I like best is this: "The zeal of the Lord Almighty will accomplish this" (Isaiah 37:32).

If you want God to rescue you, you need to pray. If He hasn't rescued you yet, you need to keep on praying! Who is the Enemy defying? You? No! He is lifting his prideful voice against God! When Sennacherib heckled the citizens of Jerusalem, he was heckling God. God defeated him to demonstrate His power over all the other gods Sennacherib had fought.

When God responded to Hezekiah's prayer in Isaiah 37:26–27, He told Hezekiah that all Sennacherib's victories were ordained by God. My dear friend, sometimes we think that God has given Satan freedom to cut loose and wreak havoc in our lives. But even when his evil schemes are leveled against you, God has whatever Satan is doing factored into His plans for your life. And when the time is right (a time that will come to you through prayer and faith), God will subdue Satan and make him return by the way that he came (Isaiah 37:34).

What will accomplish victory in your life? The zeal of the Lord Almighty! God declared that He would defend Jerusalem and save her—for His sake and for the sake of David—a great king and servant of God (Isaiah 37:35).

Let me make this observation. If you are being attacked by the enemies of God—the spirits of darkness—then your victory is assured because God's name and every promise He's made through the ages is at stake. God used an angel to kill 185,000 men in the Assyrian camp while they were sleeping! God has power over anything and everything that has power over you. Later on, when Sennacherib was back in Assyria, he was killed by his own sons when he went into the temple to worship his god.

Conclusion

I think I like Hezekiah's story because it is real, honest, and authentic. Hezekiah wasn't like so many people—he didn't bring this crisis on himself. Unlike his father, Hezekiah was a good king. He did what was right in the sight of God, and even then Sennacherib came against him.

When Sennacherib came, Hezekiah still did what was right—but while Hezekiah was professing faith in God, God remained silent and Sennacherib kept on heckling him. This is what happens with me when I am making my way through the confusing, distressing, and sometimes painful circumstances of my life. I trust God, I tell others how much I believe in Him, and still the Enemy continues to heckle.

So—when you are navigating crazy and you feel like Hezekiah when Sennacherib added insult to injury, do what Hezekiah did: Find a prayer partner and PUSH (Pray Until Something Happens)!

Treasure Hunt

Personal Reflections

- Read Hezekiah's story for yourself in 2 Kings 18–19; 2 Chronicles 32; and Isaiah 36–37.
- How would you have felt had you been Hezekiah when Sennacherib's officers starting shouting at your people?
- On what would you base your appeal to God? On what would you base your faith?
- Thank God for sharing this story with you at this moment in your life. Call out to Him and trust Him to do for you what He did for Hezekiah.

Discussion Questions

1. Have you ever found yourself in the middle of crazy? How did it feel? What did you do?
2. In what ways does the Enemy heckle your faith? What thoughts does he use against you?
3. Has God ever come through for you in an incredible way? If so, share that with your friends.
4. What part of this chapter speaks most to you?
5. Do you have a prayer partner? If not, consider getting one and praying through whatever you are facing in your life today.

Treasure Verse

When I felt secure, I said, "I will never be shaken." Lord, when you favored me, you made my royal mountain stand firm; *but when you hid your face, I was dismayed.*

Psalm 30:6–7

9

Where Was God When the Disciples Were in the Boat?

A furious squall came up, and the waves broke over the boat, so
that it was nearly swamped.

Mark 4:37

A few years ago I went on an adventure with my daughter Mikel,
her friend Kimberly, and a boatload of friends we were visiting in the Bahamas. Mikel had just graduated from high school,
and we went to Spanish Wells, Bahamas, for her senior trip. Our
adventure started at 6 a.m. when we pulled away from the dock in
our overloaded boat to head to what our friends called "the keys."
Two hours later we were in the deep blue sea trolling for dolphin
(not the kind you swim with but the blue-green kind that you eat).

Before we finished fishing, a squall surrounded us on all sides. We
had no choice but to head home right through the crashing waves
and piercing rain. By "crashing waves" I'm talking about waves that
came over the bow of the boat, smacked us in our faces, and soaked
through our waterproof jackets. Mikel and Kimberly took their seats
right in the bow of the boat. Our Bahamian friends suggested they
might be more comfortable down on the floor, but they insisted on
sitting up where they could see. And from their seats they fearlessly

faced each soaking wave with squeals of delight. When the rain pelted us, they put their diving masks on and started singing a song Ms. Anita had taught them in children's church (complete with hand motions). They were fun to watch and I wished I could have captured them on video, but it was too wet to risk pulling the camera out.

Perhaps their bravery was simple ignorance. I wish I could have been as naïve. I, on the other hand, was holding on for dear life and studying the faces of my Bahamian friends to determine if I should be more afraid than I already was. Though my friends looked concerned, they didn't look disconcerted. This was just an ordinary squall, the kind they'd braved before. We were soaked when we arrived at the dock safe and sound.

Often our misconceptions are made worse by the devil's deceptions. In the past, one of my greatest misconceptions has been that I subconsciously expected to avoid life's storms, especially with Jesus in my boat. But the story that I'm about to share with you from Mark 4:35–41 (read it for yourself) ought to clear up any confusion on the matter. If you live long enough you're going to experience squalls. Storms are inevitable. Life and waves and torrential rain and thunder and lightning and even hurricane-force winds are going to happen. Sometimes storms hit while we're in our boats. And sometimes we're in our boats because Jesus invited us there. This is where Jesus' disciples found themselves in the story we're going to study as we ask these questions: *Where was God when the disciples were in the storm? And where is He when I'm in mine?*

Let Us Go to the Other Side

As the sun was setting after a very long day of teaching a crowd of people gathered by the lake, Jesus said to His disciples, "Let us go over to the other side" (Mark 4:35). The disciples did what they always did—they followed Jesus.

Leaving the crowd behind, they took him along, just as he was, in the boat.

Mark 4:36

If you look back at Mark 4:1–2, you discover that Jesus had been teaching the crowd for quite a while, and He was tired. He wanted to get away from them and be alone with His disciples. Don't miss this gem. Jesus loves the church—we are His bride. And He meets us when we gather together to worship Him—oh, how sweet it is when Jesus meets us in places where we are gathered. But can you imagine the intimacy, the conversation, and the camaraderie that came to the disciples when they got to be with Jesus all alone? How do we experience intimate time with Jesus today? In our quiet times! But also in our homes with our families as we share what God is teaching us. And in our relationships with our dearest friends when we share what God is showing us in our lives. It is in the quiet, alone times that Jesus explains things to us. If you will get in your boat and go away to a quiet place with Jesus, He will "explain everything" to you. Look at Mark 4:33–34:

With many similar parables Jesus spoke the word to them, as much as they could understand. He did not say anything to them without using a parable. But when he was alone with his own disciples, he *explained everything*.

Getting in the boat with Jesus led to a storm, but just because storms might come, don't miss the invitation to get in the boat with Jesus. I'd rather be in the boat with Jesus than left behind on the shore, wouldn't you?

A Furious Squall

So the disciples set out to go "over to the other side" in a fishing boat with Jesus. I couldn't help but wonder what this boat might have looked like. Was it a big ship? Or a little row boat? I Googled "ancient fishing boat" (you might want to do that too) and found a boat about the size of three row boats, with raised edges and curved ends. Having been in a motorized boat on the ocean in the middle of a squall, I can say that the disciples' fishing boat would not be the kind of vessel I'd want to be in if a storm were brewing.

One of the things I love about God's Word is that it always tells me the truth. The storm the disciples encountered was not a gentle spring rain. Mark described it as a "furious squall." *Furious* is an emotional word to describe a body of water. Have you ever seen an "angry sea"? I was visiting the beach one year when the edges of a hurricane barely skimmed our waters. The beach was roped off, security guards were placed at all the boardwalks, and the water rose right to the boardwalk edges and swallowed up miles of the sandy beaches where we'd walked just days before. Because of the hurricane, the beach was a dangerous place. The angry sea threatened to breach its boundaries.

I've already told you about the "furious squall" I found myself in a few years ago in the Bahamas. One of the hardest parts of the squall is not the water coming down from the sky, but the waves that pitch your vessel and the water that pours over the edges of your craft. If you've ever experienced a furious squall up close and personal, you're probably shuddering right now from the memory of it. I've no doubt that when we get to sit down with Jesus' disciples in heaven and talk to them about their experiences walking with Him on earth, they will remember it too.

A furious squall came up, and the waves broke over the boat, so that it was nearly swamped.

Mark 4:37

So there you have it. At Jesus' suggestion, the disciples got into that boat, set out for the other side of the lake, and found themselves smack-dab in the middle of a furious squall. They never would have been in this situation in the first place had they not gone where Jesus told them to go. Following Jesus led the disciples into a storm. So where was Jesus during the storm?

> Jesus was in the stern, sleeping on a cushion.
>
> Mark 4:38

Jesus was curled up in the back of the boat sound asleep. Of course if He was in the boat that appeared on my computer screen when I Googled it, He would've been soaking wet and tossed about. There is no way He could have escaped the torrential rain and monster waves. What does this tell you about Jesus? If He could sleep through a storm like this, He was apparently exhausted. But not only that, if Jesus could sleep through a storm like this, He trusted God and knew that no matter what happened in the middle of the lake, He was going to the other side.

Don't You Care If We Drown?

As the disciples were tossed from one side to the other of their fishing boat, as some of them were bailing water, those nearest to their Lord shook Him and shouted, "Teacher, don't you care if we drown?" (Mark 4:38).

Isn't that most often our first response to the squalls in our lives? We set out to follow Jesus, being careful to obey the instructions we heard Him give us, and then a furious squall threatens our tiny vessel. Just as soon as the wind and waves toss us about we cry out, "Lord, don't you care?"

"How could I be in this storm? I was in the boat with Jesus!"

"How, Lord, could you let this happen to me?"

I want to let you in on a little secret: I don't know what storm might be tossing your boat; I don't know what hurricane winds might be causing the waves to pour over the sides of your vessel;

126

but whatever is causing the angry sea to threaten you is not happening *to you*. It is just happening! When my husband preached a message on this passage of Scripture, he made a point that some of us miss. Jesus' boat wasn't the only one in the water that night. There were other boats being tossed about too (see Mark 4:36). Life just happens. It's a mean, angry, and sometimes furious squall, but don't get confused amidst the chaos. When squalls come your way, God has not decided to just zero in on you. He didn't cast you off into the deep just so He could unleash His fury and shake up your world. Seas get angry, and squalls happen.

Doubt and Fear

I'm fortunate to have been taken to church as a child, and I'm old enough to have been reared on the old hymns. There is one hymn that seems to go hand in hand with this story. It has these words in it:

> Standing on the promises that cannot fail,
>   when the howling storms of doubt and fear assail.
> By the living word of God I shall prevail.
> Standing on the promises of God!
>
> Standing, standing, standing on the promises of God my
>   Savior;
> standing, standing, I'm standing on the promises of God![1]

The phrase I like is "When the howling storms of doubt and fear assail." I got to thinking about doubt and fear—and realized that doubt fuels fear, and fear feeds doubt. These two are interchangeable and interlinked. If fear and doubt are interchangeable, I am led to believe that if I can somehow remove my doubt, then

1. Russell K. Carter, "Standing on the Promises," 1886. Public Domain

I can overcome my fear. Which do you suppose is easier to deal with—your fear or your doubt?

Doubt is birthed in your mind. When your thoughts are troubled, when what you expect doesn't happen, or when circumstances challenge your beliefs, you begin to doubt. This is what happened to the disciples. Before the waves rocked their little boat, the disciples were more than ready to follow Jesus. They fully anticipated arriving at the other side of the lake rested and ready. But then the squall unleashed its fury. Had Jesus changed? No, Jesus was still the same in the storm as He was before the storm. What had changed was the sea. The circumstances that the disciples found themselves in changed, and those soaking waves on that angry sea caused the disciples to doubt God. Has that ever happened to you?

It has happened to me. I told you of our soaking waves in the introduction to this book. But if you're like me and skipped over that part, I'll just mention them again. In a matter of a year I was diagnosed with cancer, and my eighteen-year-old daughter, Mikel, left our family, moved in with her boyfriend, got pregnant, and had a baby girl. That same year our church was flooded, my husband had skin cancer on his eyelid and surgery to remove it, my son got sick with mono, and my other daughter was diagnosed with polycystic ovarian syndrome (the same infertility issue I had twenty-plus years ago). I was following God's voice as clearly as I'd ever heard it and was writing *Spiritual Warfare for Women*. I cried out to God, shook Him awake, and shouted, "Don't you care if we drown?" My doubts were birthed in the uncertainty created by the circumstances of life that were pouring over the sides of my boat. Life's experiences can do that to us.

Quiet! Be Still!

Doubt fueled fear and fear fed doubt when that furious squall threatened the lives of Jesus' disciples. Mark 4:39 is perhaps one of my favorite verses in the Bible. I love this verse because as soon as Jesus woke up, He got up. And as soon as Jesus got up, He spoke up to the disciples' circumstances:

Quiet! Be still!

The Creator, who tells the ocean its boundaries, spoke to the waves and made them be still. God has power like that over your circumstances too. Many times this past year, as I have tried to make my way through the waves that seem to never cease, Jesus got up, rebuked the wind, and said to the waves, "Quiet! Be still!" I've kept a record of some of the times He's done this on a calendar. For every day that Jesus spoke peace to my storm, I recorded the events of that day. My calendar is full of evidence that Jesus kept the storm at bay.

But after Jesus rebuked the wind and the waves, He asked His disciples two questions:

1. Why are you so afraid?
2. Do you still have no faith?

If I had been one of Jesus' disciples, and if I hadn't remembered my manners, I might have wanted to respond to Jesus' questions, "Are you kidding me? Why am I afraid? Because those waves were drowning me!" And if I'd heard my Master rebuke my faith, out of indignation and frustration I might have wanted to shout, "How am I supposed to conjure up faith when you are sleeping and I am stuck in this boat in an angry sea that is far beyond my ability to control?"

Come on, be honest. Might you have wanted to respond in that way too? When you find yourself in a furious squall, it is reasonable to be afraid. Furious squalls have a way of instilling fear, and fear has a way of leading even the most trusting child to doubt her heavenly Father's love.

But remember what Jesus said to His disciples earlier that day when evening came:

Let us go over to the other side.

Mark 4:35

Jesus told His disciples they were going to the other side. If Jesus told you that you are headed to the other side, there's not a storm fierce enough to keep you away! You're gonna make it. Whatever waves are tossing your boat, those waves will not do you in. Jesus will see you through.

They Were Terrified

Mark 4:41 says that the disciples were terrified after all this happened, and they asked each other, "Who is this?" Haven't your circumstances left you asking the same thing? "Who is this?" With every furious squall, there is the opportunity to learn something more about the divine nature of God. I haven't learned all that He means for me to learn, but I am an eager student.

Today I know that God gave my family the ability to love and forgive and love again over and over as often as is required of us. My husband and I, and my daughter and her husband (the son-in-law I thought I never wanted), have learned the power of love. Today we are a family who is learning to love one another in a way that reflects the unconditional love of God. We are learning to respect the free will He gives each of us. In the midst of our tempest, God brought us our granddaughter. If you ever have the privilege of meeting her, you will have to agree with me that she is the happiest little person on earth. She loves people, especially her family, and she shares her generous joy with whomever she encounters. That precious girl whose conception caused my furious squall is now my deepest joy.

My friends, if God has said you are going to the other side—you are going to the other side! He alone knows how you'll get there—and He alone will see you through.

Where Was God When the Disciples Were in the Boat?

Where was God when the disciples were in the boat? He was right there with them, confident that He would see them through. Where is God when your boat is being tossed about? He's right there with you, eager to show you how much He loves you. He is right there with you, challenging your faith and giving you courage. Had the storm not raged, the disciples wouldn't have had an a-ha moment with Jesus. Sometimes God lets the storms rage so that we can be reminded that He is Lord of the waves.

Treasure Hunt

No matter the strength of the wind, the force of the waves, or the pelting of the rain, with Jesus in the boat you will get to the other side.

Personal Reflection

- Read Mark 4:35–41.
- Try to put yourself in that boat with Jesus' disciples. What would you have thought, how would you have felt, while Jesus was sleeping?
- What would you have thought, how would you have felt, when He got up and calmed the waves?
- Consider the last time you went through a storm. What blessings might you have missed had you not experienced that furious squall?

Discussion Questions

1. Find a picture of a fishing boat like the one that Jesus and His disciples were in the night this storm took place. Show that picture and share with one another what you might have thought and felt had you been in that boat.

2. Share a time when you were caught in a furious squall either physically (on a boat in the water) or figuratively (in your life). Share how God met you there. What did you learn about His nature and His love?

3. Do you believe that God can calm your storm? Why or why not? Would you be willing to ask Him to? Pray with one another and ask God to be glorified (which simply means to express exactly what His power and love are capable of doing) in your storms.

Treasure Verse

He got up, rebuked the wind and said to the waves, "Quiet! Be still!" Then the wind died down and it was completely calm.

Mark 4:39

PART THREE

Let God Define Good

Doubt swallows faith partially because of the way many Christians define what is and what is not "good." We have a tendency to plan out the good in ours and our loved ones' lives. We decide that going to college after high school is good. We decide that getting a job that pays well right after college is good. Buying a car, owning a house, getting married, and a few years later starting our families is all good, good, good, and good! We have it all planned out. Then when something happens that is not good—say, our children don't go to college but join the army instead, or we're diagnosed with cancer, or our husband runs off with another woman, or our mother has Alzheimer's, or . . . When those things happen we fret, we worry, we cry out to God, and we question His goodness and His love. What might happen if we let God define good?

> Restlessness and impatience change nothing except our peace and joy. Peace does not dwell in outward things, but in the heart prepared to wait trustfully and quietly on Him who has all things safely in His hands.[1]
>
> —Elisabeth Elliot

1. Elisabeth Elliot, *Keep a Quiet Heart* (Ann Arbor, MI: Servant Publications, 1995), 135.

10

From Hope-So to Know-So Faith

> "'If you can'?" said Jesus. "Everything is possible for one who believes."
>
> Mark 9:23

There is a great big difference between hope-so and know-so faith. Hope-so faith believes God hears us when we cry and that He is able to answer our prayers. Know-so faith trusts that He will. The story we're going to examine in this chapter shows the difference between these two.

The Day the Disciples Failed

The day the disciples failed was the same day that Jesus took Peter, James, and John with Him to a high mountain where He was "transfigured" before them. We're not going to talk about the transfiguration, but oh, how amazing it must have been to have seen Jesus in all His glory! It's the way we will see Him when we first lay eyes on Him in heaven.

The story we are going to discuss comes out of Mark 9:14–19. When Jesus, James, John, and Peter returned to the other disciples, they found them in the midst of a large crowd and engaged in a heated debate with the religious leaders. What a smack back into the reality of this chaos we call life on earth. Several years ago my church hosted weekend retreats for women. We began our retreats on Friday nights and concluded them at lunch on Saturday. I'll never forget how many of the women wanted to linger at those retreats because they weren't quite ready for what would be waiting for them at home. James, John, and Peter might have shared their sentiment. Just after their great mountaintop experience, they returned to "normal" life . . . life where the power of God is challenged and the reality of God is questioned.

When they came to where the other disciples were, they saw a large crowd gathered to hear an argument between the religious leaders and Jesus' other disciples. A distraught father was caught in the mayhem with his demon-possessed boy. Mark 9:15 says, "As soon as all the people saw Jesus, they were overwhelmed with wonder and ran to greet him." The HCSB says "they were amazed." I love this! The people were excited to see Jesus because they knew that something was about to happen simply because Jesus had shown up. Most likely that crowd ran to greet Jesus, and everyone talked at once. When you show up in the middle of a mess, those in the mess all want to tell you what's going on, and they all want to talk at the same time. In order to understand what was going on, Jesus asked His disciples, "What are you arguing with them about?" But the disciples didn't answer Him; another man did.

> A man in the crowd answered, "Teacher, I brought you my son, who is possessed by a spirit that has robbed him of speech. Whenever it seizes him, it throws him to the ground. He foams at the mouth, gnashes his teeth and becomes rigid. I asked your disciples to drive out the spirit, but they could not."
>
> Mark 9:17–18

Notice that desperate need trumps theological debate *every* time. The disciples might have been frustrated because they couldn't perform a miracle; the religious rulers might have been satisfied because they had opportunity to argue their point; but this father was brokenhearted. He didn't come to "church" that day to argue about why God would or wouldn't answer his prayer. He came to find Jesus because his son needed help. And while Jesus' disciples and the religious leaders argued, this man's grief consumed him. No amount of debate was going to heal his boy.

Notice that the father was not nearly as concerned about the failure of Jesus' disciples as he was with his own son's desperate need. Look at Mark 9:17 again. The father told Jesus why he came: "I brought you my son, who is possessed by a spirit that has robbed him of speech." Then he described what his boy suffered: "Whenever it seizes him, it throws him to the ground. He foams at the mouth, gnashes his teeth and becomes rigid." And after that, the father stated the problem, "I asked your disciples to drive out the spirit, but they could not." This father didn't want to know *why* Jesus' disciples couldn't heal his boy. He just wanted Jesus to answer his cry for help.

Most often people come to church for the same reason today. They want to meet Jesus; they need to meet Jesus. Heartaches drive us to Jesus way more than arguments, persuasive speech, or even beautiful music. Can you imagine how this father felt when the disciples failed to cast the demon out of his son? Can you imagine how it might have felt like rubbing salt in the wound when their failure led to a religious argument? How tragic that we sometimes get sidetracked with arguments that make no difference at all to the wounded masses. How very tragic it is that those arguments cause us to completely miss the brokenhearted people who've come our way hungry for an encounter with the living Lord!

Michael Catt writes this:

Maybe your situation is nowhere near the extent of this one, but you are defeated nonetheless. Satan uses you like a punching bag. Just about the time you think you've got your act together, he karate chops you and knocks you to the ground. You feel beaten, battered, and bruised, emotionally you don't know if you can take it anymore; mentally it's draining the life out of you; spiritually you wonder if God even cares.

Maybe you have been disappointed by God's people, by the church or by a minister. The nine disciples were unable to help. It wasn't a lack of desire that hindered the nine; it was a lack of faith. God's people will disappoint you because they are frail flesh just like you are. God's servants aren't perfect. If your desperation leads you to curse the church or the servants of God, it's because you've put your faith and hope in men and institutions rather than in the Lord God of heaven.[1]

It's important to understand that disciples sometimes fail. But it's just as important to remember that Jesus never fails.

Jesus' Reaction to the Disciples' Predicament

Once Jesus heard the father's cry, He immediately rebuked His disciples rather harshly. In fact, He called the entire generation "unbelieving": "You unbelieving generation," Jesus replied, "how long shall I stay with you?" (Mark 9:19). As a mother, have you ever said anything similar? I have! "What were you thinking?" "Could you make life any more difficult for yourself?" "How long do you intend to think this way?"

It is interesting that Jesus didn't let His disciples off the hook. He could have said, "Oh, bless your hearts. I wasn't here and you were just confused. It'll be okay; I'm here now and will make everything better." No! Jesus tongue-lashed them right there in front

1. Michael Catt, *MasterWork: Essential Messages from God's Servants* (Nashville, TN: Lifeway Christian Resources, Summer 2011), 58.

of the crowd and the religious rulers. From the sounds of it, He was sincerely disturbed that His disciples were unable to cast this demon out. What is the take-away for us? Jesus expects us to grow up and become like Him. He expects us to take authority over the Enemy and defeat him. We are not called to live our lives arguing over why we have no power in our faith. We are expected to minister with the same power Jesus had. He expects us not only to do what He did, but to do greater things as well. He told us this was His expectation in John 14.

> I tell you the truth, anyone who believes in me will do the same works I have done, and even greater works, because I am going to be with the Father.
>
> John 14:12 NLT

There's no whining in following Jesus! We serve a living Savior, and we are expected to deliver the same healing and hope that He delivered. But why don't we? Are we guilty of the lack of faith that Jesus rebuked in His disciples? Notice that Jesus didn't rebuke His disciples for their lack of desire, their erroneous miracle-working methods, or their weak compassion. He rebuked them for their lack of faith. The disciples wanted to help that father. They most likely hurt for him. They wanted to represent Jesus well—they'd given up everything to follow Him! But they were unable to heal this boy because they lacked *faith*. Perhaps that is our problem today.

A Lesson in Faith

What I really love about this story is how Jesus taught a lesson in faith. In the same breath, He rebuked His disciples for their unbelief and told the distraught father to bring Him his son (Mark 9:19).

If I had been that dad, my heart would have started racing. The Scripture says they brought the boy to Jesus, and when the spirit saw Him, it immediately acted out, throwing the boy into a convulsion. As the boy rolled on the ground, foaming at the mouth, Jesus asked the father a question.

How long has he been like this?

Mark 9:21

It's a question of concern and compassion. I bet this boy's father had tears in his eyes when he told Jesus that his son had been tormented by this evil spirit ever since he was a young child. He went on to add that sometimes the spirit had thrown the boy into fire and water in attempts to kill him. Imagine that! The father had most likely reached into flames to rescue his son. They probably both had terrible scars from the burns. And there were most likely other times when the father had risked his own life to rescue his son from swift waters where the spirit had tossed his convulsing body. With the weight of these memories, and the agony of the years, the father prayed a most desperate prayer:

But if you can do anything, take pity on us and help us.

Mark 9:22

Perhaps that morning the father was certain Jesus could heal his boy. Maybe when he left his home and went to where he'd heard Jesus' disciples were seen, he harbored hope and joyful anticipation. But standing in the middle of the crowd after experiencing the disciples' failure and watching his son writhe in pain, those hopes were dashed and only a tiny thread of faith remained. It's no wonder his heart's cry was prefaced with an "if."

But it just happened to be that "if" that Jesus picked up on. "'If you can'?" said Jesus. "Everything is possible for him who believes."

Oh, these are the exact words that bother me! How many times do I pray "If you can" kind of prayers? How often do I neglect to consider that "everything is possible for him who believes"? Just the other morning I was having this discussion with the Lord. My

140

cancer is being treated with chemotherapy now (as I'm writing this book). I've just finished two rounds of treatment and will have either eight or ten more. It's not pleasant—not pleasant at all. But there is no longer any traceable cancer in my body, and my doctor is hopeful that with chemotherapy I will never have cancer ever again. However, there is a man in our church whose cancer is scattered throughout his body. He was diagnosed with the same cancer as me two years ago, just after we discovered mine. In those two years he's fought a great fight, but his tumors are still present. And to make matters worse, just two weeks ago his twenty-year-old son was diagnosed with the exact same cancer, and his cancer had spread from his colon to his liver and his brain.

I was thinking about Gail, a great woman of faith who is even more desperate than the father in Mark 9, for both her husband and her son are in a fight for their lives. My prayer went something like this. I sensed God ask me, "Leighann, do you believe that I can heal little cancer?" (By little cancer, I was thinking about mine.) I answered right away, "Yes, Lord. I believe you can heal my cancer. In fact, I believe that you will!" But before I could be satisfied with my expression of faith, God then asked this, "Do you believe I can heal big cancer?" (By big cancer, I was thinking about Kim and Taylor, the men who are suffering much more advanced cancer in their bodies.) I didn't answer right away because I knew that God knew my hesitation. But as He patiently waited for my response, I reasoned in my mind, *Doesn't all healing power come from the Lord? Didn't He make us? Doesn't He heal us?* I've had several surgeries and have been amazed throughout both experiences in the miraculous healing power that flows through my body without any real work from anyone. The doctors can remove tumors, but they can't heal the wound; God does that. The doctors can administer chemotherapy, but they can't restore the body; God does that. So I carefully answered, "Lord, only you heal. You are the God who heals." And then God asked me to remember what He said in

His Word: "What is impossible with man is possible with God" (Luke 18:27). And I said, "Amen."

So with my little bitty faith, as honest as I can, I am praying for the complete and total healing of my friends with big cancer. I was reminded by a fellow chemo friend that it's "just" cancer. And that cancer in no way usurps or rules over God in our lives. Even as I tell you this story, I feel like the demon-possessed boy's father, who said, "I do believe; help me overcome my unbelief!"

What a beautiful prayer! "Lord, I do believe; help me overcome my unbelief!" But what is even more beautiful is the way Jesus answered that prayer.

> When Jesus saw that a crowd was running to the scene, he rebuked the impure spirit. "You deaf and mute spirit," he said, "I command you, come out of him and never enter him again."
>
> Mark 9:25

The spirit had no choice but to obey. For in the realm of the heavenly powers, Jesus rules supreme. Mark records that the spirit shrieked, convulsed the boy violently, and came out. The boy was so still once the spirit was gone that the crowd thought he was dead.

> But Jesus took him by the hand and lifted him to his feet, and he stood up.
>
> Mark 9:27

Isn't that great? To help this boy's father with his unbelief, Jesus performed a miracle and answered his heart's most desperate cry. That's the kind of faith-building experience I want to have!

No Prayer = No Power

Later, when Jesus' disciples were all alone and away from the crowds, they asked Him, "Why couldn't we drive [that demon] out [of that boy]?" Jesus told them that their powerlessness was directly linked to their prayerlessness. That is all that He said: "This kind can come out only by prayer" (Mark 9:28–29).

Last night I was struggling with a burden for someone I love. I had been thinking of her on and off all day long, even had dreams about her the night before. Sometimes when that happens I take it as a call to prayer. As I piddled about trying to write a bit on this book, I kept thinking about going to my room and spending some time in prayer. But I put off the urge. Later, after I'd crawled into bed and started reading, the thought came again that I ought to spend time praying for my friend. I put my book down and began to pray.

While I was praying I realized that thinking about, wanting, daydreaming, and even talking about how God might "fix" a situation is not the same as praying. Perhaps we fail to experience the miraculous and the impossible because we do not pray. The next time you are challenged to take God at His Word, spend some time in prayer. Tell God what is on your heart and mind and then remind Him of what He's said to you. A great place to start is Mark 9:23: "Everything is possible for one who believes."

Treasure Hunt

Personal Reflections

- Read the biblical account of this story in Mark 9:14–29.
- Put yourself in the sandals of Jesus' disciples. How might it feel to fail to perform a miracle in front of your hecklers? How might it feel to see Jesus headed your way?
- Put yourself in the sandals of the father with the demon-possessed son. How would you feel if Jesus' disciples couldn't heal your boy? How would you feel when you saw Jesus headed your way?

• When is the last time that you wanted to pray like that father: "Lord, I believe! Help my unbelief!"?

Discussion Questions

1. Ask three people to pretend to be the following persons and tell the story in their own words: one of the religious leaders, one of Jesus' disciples, and the father of the boy who was demon possessed.
2. Share a time in your life when you wanted to pray like that boy's father prayed. How did God answer your prayer?
3. What is the difference between thinking about prayer and praying? How do you spend time in prayer?
4. Consider spending fifteen minutes in prayer with one another. Keep a record of the ways that God responds to the prayers of your group.

Treasure Verse

Jesus replied, "What is impossible with man is possible with God."

Luke 18:27

11

God Is Bigger Than This

Do you not know? Have you not heard? The Lord is the everlasting God, the Creator of the ends of the earth. He will not grow tired or weary, and his understanding no one can fathom. He gives strength to the weary and increases the power of the weak.

Isaiah 40:28–29

One of the privileges of being a pastor's wife is that I get to have a front-row seat in the lives of people as they go through all kinds of trials. I love this aspect of the ministry; for when the prince of this world lashes out with his terrible blows, God's children are put in a place where God proves himself faithful and true. The hard part is trusting Him when He seems to be sitting idly by, letting the devil have a heyday with us. We know that "all things work together for good," but we have a hard time really believing the truth of that statement when things are working together regardless. I hope that by sharing the following story from one of many in my years of ministry you will be encouraged to hold on tight as you wait for God to come through for you.

Melissa's Miracle

My friend Melissa has a great big personality and a voice to match it. She's from Texas and is every bit the Texas woman—big hair, big ideas, big hugs, and big life! She's the kind of person who makes people smile when she walks into a room. She finds an excuse for a party quicker than ants find food at a picnic! When she and her husband lived in Thompson Station, she was one of the featured soloists at our church. Tom absolutely loved to hear her sing, and Melissa loved to sing.

I am the prayer minister at our church. Part of my role as the prayer minister is to be sensitive to the spiritual atmosphere of our congregation and call our people to prayer in response to the things that go on. One year our church was bombarded by an unusual attack on marriages—more so than normal. Men and women who were serving in leadership were experiencing difficulty in their marriages that they'd never had before. I was burdened by this attack, and as I prayed I became incensed. How dare the Enemy come into the halls of our church and wreak havoc amongst us! I decided to issue a call to prayer specifically for marriages.

So on Mother's Day I stood before the congregation with far less courage than I felt in my quiet time. With my knees shaking, I issued a challenge to the men to be spiritual leaders and to commit to pray with their wives every day between Mother's Day and Father's Day. It was a period of seven weeks that husbands and wives would bow their heads together and pray. I asked the husbands to come to the altar, print their email addresses on index cards, and commit to this challenge. I had no idea how the couples in our church would respond to my challenge. Tom endorsed the call to prayer, and then we sang a song. Hundreds of men immediately left their seats and flooded to the altar. Over three hundred couples committed to pray together daily for their marriages and their families. That was in 2005. Since then we've observed a season of prayer for marriages every year that begins on Mother's Day and concludes on Father's Day. We call this season of prayer CPR, Couples Praying Regardless.

When I went back to my own prayers the week after I issued the challenge, I was thrilled with the congregation's response. But I felt an urge to tell a really big story on Father's Day. I wanted God to give us a fireworks kind of testimony, one that shouted the glory of God when His people pray. Already people were emailing me stories of the ways that God was working as they were praying, and I just knew that God was going to use this opportunity to really show off.

A few weeks after that, Melissa invited me to lunch. Now, I knew that David and Melissa had been praying a long time for a baby. Melissa suffered infertility, and Tom and I were fervently praying for her to have a child. I also knew that she and David were struggling in their marriage. I didn't know much about the details of their situation, but I knew enough to consider them one of our great couples who were under attack. Besides being a featured soloist in our worship ministry, she and her husband also led a small group for young married couples. Theirs was certainly not the only marriage under attack, and theirs was not one that I had been involved in through counseling. But I knew Melissa well enough to know that she might be frustrated with me for proclaiming in front of the church that our marriages were being bombarded by the Enemy, so I was a bit anxious about our lunch date.

Sure enough, after our salads were served, Melissa confronted me by saying, "Leighann, I have to admit that when you told the church that marriages were under attack, I thought to myself, *You might as well put a picture of me and David on the big screens.*" I smiled and assured her that although I knew they were going through a difficult time, they were not the only ones, and they were not even the ones I was thinking of when I spoke. I'm not sure she believed me, but she continued, "I want you to know that David and I have been praying every day. And I want to give a testimony."

I was thrilled. If Melissa and David were willing to stand in front of the church and testify, our congregation would be so encouraged. And then she continued, "For the first time in a long time David and I prayed, and we didn't pray about a baby. Instead we prayed about us, our marriage, and what God wants in our lives." How cool was that? I was so excited. She went on, "And through those prayers God is healing our marriage." Yeah, I knew I was going to have my fireworks on Father's Day.

But Melissa wasn't finished. "And guess what . . ."

"What?" I couldn't imagine more.

"I'm pregnant."

Oh my goodness! We'd been praying for Melissa to conceive a baby for a very long time, and now, smack-dab in the middle of our brave challenge to the couples to pray, and trust God, and see what only He can do, my infertile friend was expecting a baby. This was good; this was very good!

"No way!" I exclaimed with a laugh.

"Yes! Pregnant, when we weren't even asking God about it." Melissa spilled over with excitement.

I told her that of course I wanted her and David to share their testimony on Father's Day. But then, a woman of faith that I am, I said this: "But, Melissa, you need to know that if you tell the congregation about your pregnancy and then lose this baby (she'd had a few miscarriages before), they will all know and you will have to deal with everyone knowing your business."

Now, before you chastise me for my lack of faith, understand that I had been a pastor's wife for a very long time and I knew what it was like to be infertile, to be pregnant, to have three babies in three years, and to suffer the embarrassment of having a child kick the door in a fit on Sunday night when I left him in child care. I knew what it was like to have hundreds of people watching me live my life every step of the way. It's not easy, and I wanted Melissa to think it through.

Melissa smiled at me and said, "If God's answered this prayer at this time, I'm going to believe that it's because He wants to get glory out of this pregnancy, and I want all the prayers I can get going through this." I smiled at Melissa's faith, celebrated her answered prayers, and went home absolutely thrilled at how God was taking care of Father's Day.

On Father's Day, David and Melissa shared their testimony, telling their church family how God had miraculously healed their hearts and then answered their cries for a child. We all celebrated and I smiled.

Miracle or Madness?

A few weeks later, Melissa called and told me that they'd been to the doctor and heard their baby's heartbeat. She was excited and I was thrilled. I *love* it when God does things like this! I thought this was the beginning of the end of a beautiful God story.

But a few months after that, I got the news that something was terribly wrong with Melissa's baby. When she and her husband went to the doctor's visit where you get to have an ultrasound and find out the sex of your child, they found out that their child had a serious condition. The baby's bladder was swollen, indicating a blockage in the urethra valve. The doctor's prognosis was grim. In fact, Melissa and David were told they could carry their baby to term with the knowledge that they would be facing death at delivery. Or they could try to put a shunt in the baby while in the womb—a very serious procedure that was more successful on boys than girls. Their third choice was to terminate the pregnancy. Of course David and Melissa wouldn't even consider terminating their God-given pregnancy. Instead, they shared the details of their nightmare with a crowd of witnesses and invited the church to pray with them that God would perform a miracle.

I'll never forget the day I heard this news. It was a beautifully sunny day and I'd just been on a walk. When I got back home and discovered Melissa's miracle child was critically ill, I knelt beside my bed and cried out to God from deep inside my soul. I told Him that if He didn't save this child, our fireworks on Father's Day would be wasted. What kind of God gives such a precious gift, then takes it away? I wrestled with how I would explain Him to our people if He didn't heal this baby. And then I simply wept. As my tears were flowing God gave me a *word*. It was as clearly spoken to my spirit as if God had spoken it aloud. He does that; when we're on our knees and desperate He gives us His *word*.

The word God gave me was Ephesians 3:20:

> Now to him who is able to do immeasurably more than all we ask or imagine, according to his power that is at work within us, to him be glory in the church and in Christ Jesus throughout all generations, forever and ever! Amen.

I looked up and took a deep sigh of relief. *That* was a good word! I smiled and then I pictured Melissa and David on Father's Day (the next year) holding up a baby girl for all the church to see. Not often does that happen to me, but during my prayer for Melissa's baby, God gave me both a word and a vision. My heart rested and I knew my prayer was done.

I can't remember if I ever told Melissa about that prayer time. But soon after I got up off my knees, I found out that she wanted us to pray and ask God that her baby be a boy. A boy had greater chances of survival in the situation he was in. So we prayed and a bit later we were elated that God heard and answered our prayers and gave us what we asked. Melissa's baby was a boy.

But then another day came with more bad news. The doctor would no longer consider the shunt procedure an option because the baby's kidneys were not functioning and his life was not considered viable. As far as the doctor was concerned, Melissa could carry her child to term, but he would not live. Melissa faithfully reported all of these things to us as we prayed with her that God would perform a miracle. We had prayer meetings and we encouraged one another to believe. We quoted Scripture, claimed promises, worshiped with lifted arms, and held God at His Word. We were relentless, not giving the Lord a moment's peace regarding our friends and their baby over the next several months.

During the holidays Melissa sent this beautiful message to the crowd of witnesses that was praying her through:

> I worried so much about sending out an email during the holidays, but so many of you have asked for an update that I hated not to respond.
>
> Sweet Elisha. What a joy it is to get to see him every two weeks on the ultrasound machine at the doctor's office. He is always there with a strong heartbeat, and man is he growing! But growth is about the only change we see in him. Elisha still has no fluid in his sac, so they say he still has no chance of having lungs that have been able to properly develop. His little bladder is anything but little considering how overextended it is (but don't worry about his being uncomfortable, God has assured me that he is not). It is completely full of fluid that he is unable to release, and last week we found out that the fluid is now backing up into his kidneys. So no, there is still no function in his kidneys. But that's enough of the bad stuff.
>
> He is, however, moving more than they said he would. He kicks and turns and flips almost every day—all through the day. Trust me on this. It was only a few weeks ago that Elisha was breech. We were told there would be no way he could move into a proper birth position before February, but just two weeks later there he was! Perfectly positioned in every way. It was the first time I have heard my doctor laugh in amazement.
>
> Mostly in this email I want you to know two things. One, is how absolutely unshaken we are in our belief that Elisha will come home with us. Call us crazy, the doctors do, we don't care. Too much prayer has gone up, too many words have been spoken, and God has set this stage too perfectly to not perform a miracle in His name. We are so thankful that during this season we get to have him so close to us. Elisha keeps me warm, in more ways than one.

Secondly, we'd like to tell you all how your friendship and prayers have changed our lives. They truly have. I could say how nice they are and how kind it is of you, but that wouldn't suffice. Some of the things you guys have prayed over us, written in cards to us, and spoken to us have truly changed our lives. If we have the level of faith that we do—some of you are to blame! Keep believing that on February 14 we all receive a miraculous gift of love.

David and I have two Scriptures that we carry around with us in our hearts every day. The first is one that scrolls through our minds every time the doctors tell us how long we will have to spend with Elisha. First Corinthians 1:19 says, "I will destroy the wisdom of the wise, and I will set aside the understanding of the experts" (HCSB).

The second one was given to me in my quiet time one day when I was, well, I'll admit it, very, very scared. I turned to Romans 4:16 and read, "This is why the fulfillment of God's promise depends entirely on trusting God and his way, and then simply embracing him and what he does. God's promise arrives as a pure gift" (THE MESSAGE).

May we all bless God with our belief!

Elisha Cooper will live, *and not die*, to declare the works of the Lord.

I agreed with her wholeheartedly, especially with this part: "God has set this stage too perfectly to not perform a miracle in His name." How could this baby die? Our entire church was praying for him to live, and we were eager to see God perform a miracle in our midst.

Christmas Day

Christmas fell on Sunday that year, and we always spent Christmas with my family in Georgia, so I'd taken our children and driven to my parents' house on Christmas Eve. Tom stayed to preach Sunday morning with plans to drive down Sunday afternoon and join us.

We'd already opened gifts early Christmas morning, and everyone was taking baths and getting dressed for the day. I was sitting in my bedroom having my quiet time. For Christmas morning, I chose Isaiah 40 as my chapter to read. I love that chapter of the Bible; it is perhaps my favorite. Somewhere around verse 11,

> "He tends his flock like a shepherd: He gathers the lambs in his arms and carries them close to his heart; he gently leads those that have young."

. . . the phone rang. My mother called up to me that Tom was on the line. I smiled, thinking that he wanted to wish me a Merry Christmas before he went to preach—it was our first Christmas morning spent apart. But when I answered the phone and heard the tone of his voice, I knew that something terrible had happened. My heart fell as it always does when you know that anything can happen to anyone at anytime. And Tom shared his news, "Leighann, David and Melissa had their baby this morning."

I interrupted (I always do), "Oh! That's too early!" (He was due on Valentine's Day.)

"Yes. He lived for an hour and died." And Tom was silent.

"Oh . . ." I wished I could be with Tom at that moment. What a heavy burden to bear on Christmas morning—to have to preach and to have to grieve and to have to be strong because everyone is watching to see what you do. I continued, "On Christmas?"

But then he told me an amazing thing. He said he'd already talked to David and Melissa and they were okay. They were worshiping and praising God for the precious gift of their precious son, and they were thankful for the hour they were able to share in his brief life.

Well, I'm just not that spiritual. My immediate thought was, *What kind of gift is that?!* But I was spiritual enough not to say it aloud. Instead I just muttered, "Huh . . ."

153

Tom told me he would be on his way down right after the service and that we'd probably have to come back home the next day for the memorial service and burial. I told him I loved him and that I was praying for him and to be careful driving. Then I went back to Isaiah 40 and my quiet time.

Later that night I got a phone call from Melissa. She sounded much stronger than I would have been had I lived the Christmas she lived that day. "Leighann, I want you to speak at Elisha's service," she said.

"You do?" I asked. "Why?"

"Well, people are going to be wondering what Elisha's short life has to do with God and prayer and I want you to explain that to them," she answered.

I replied honestly, "Melissa, I'm kind of wondering those things too. But I would be honored to speak at Elisha's service. I love you and I am so sorry."

Elisha's Memorial Service

The day came for us to bury David and Melissa's miracle baby. Funerals for babies are always so sad. We'd just had one a few weeks before this, and while we stood over baby Elisha's grave, I could still see the fresh grave of that tiny baby girl. I can't remember what the weather was like that day. My heart was so sad for Melissa and David, and I stood with them and their family in awe of their strength and their resolve to be completely submitted to God's rule and reign in their lives.

That night we had Elisha Cooper Radke's memorial service. Tom delivered an amazing message from Psalm 118.

I was pushed back and about to fall, but the Lord helped me. The Lord is my strength and my defense; he has become my salvation.

Psalm 118:13–14

My grieving husband assured Melissa that she would sing again. Then it was my turn. Here are the notes I used when I spoke at Elisha's memorial service:

Elisha Cooper Radke and Prayer

December 27, 2005

> Prepare the way of the Lord; make straight in the desert a highway for our God. Every valley shall be exalted and every mountain and hill brought low; the crooked places shall be made straight and the rough places smooth; the glory of the Lord shall be revealed, and all flesh shall see it together.
>
> Isaiah 40:3–5 NJKV

Isaiah 40—This is what I was reading in my quiet time on Christmas morning when Tom called me at my parents' house in Powder Springs, Georgia. I love this chapter in the Bible. I'm considering memorizing the entire thing. These verses speak of what I consider my ministry to be. In urging people toward praying and believing God to do what only He can do, I see my role as making straight a highway for God—removing the valleys of despair and courageously conquering the mountains of impossibility so that together we can experience the glory of the Lord as it is revealed.

Tom said, "David and Melissa had Elisha. They held him for an hour and then he died." The first words out of my mouth were "On Christmas?" To which Tom quickly replied, "They consider it their gift from God!" And I didn't say a word. Tears welled in my eyes and I fought something like anger bubbling in my soul—and since I was in Isaiah 40 I read on . . .

> Who has measured the waters in the hollow of his hand, or with the breadth of his hand marked off the heavens? Who has held the dust of the earth in a basket, or weighed the mountains on the scales and the hills in a balance? Who can fathom the Spirit of the Lord, or instruct the Lord as his counselor?
>
> Isaiah 40:12–13

155

And I closed my quiet time with this: "Certainly not me. Amen."

Like you—all of you who love David and Melissa so much—I continued Christmas with a certain sorrow mingled with the joy and wonder of the day. At lunch Mikel and Kaleigh were talking about our plans for this week, and I told them that Daddy (who was on his way right then to be with us) and I would be coming back home today for a funeral. Of course they wanted to know who died. So I said, "Mrs. Melissa had baby Elisha today. He lived for an hour and died."

Together Mikel and Kaleigh said, "On Christmas?!" And I quickly replied, "Oh, but David and Melissa consider Elisha a gift from God and an answer to their prayer!"

I really tried to sound full of hope and understanding. But one of the girls—I can't remember which one put into words what I'd been trying desperately *not* to think all morning—said, "Answered prayer! Some answered prayer this is! How could God give them their baby and then let him die?"

It felt good to get those words out in the air! I immediately told them those were my thoughts exactly.

Oh God, if you've called me to make a way in the wilderness for people to come to you—how on earth am I to raise this valley up and bring this mountain low? You've got to work with me here! And I remembered the rest of Isaiah 40 . . .

Do you not know? Have you not heard? Has it not been told you from the beginning? Have you not understood since the earth was founded? He sits enthroned above the circle of the earth, and its people are like grasshoppers. He stretches out the heavens like a canopy, and spreads them out like a tent to live in. He brings princes to naught and reduces the rulers of this world to nothing. . . .

"To whom will you compare me? Or who is my equal?" says the Holy One. Lift your eyes and look to the heavens: Who created all these? He who brings out the starry host one by one and calls forth each of them by name. Because of his great power and mighty strength, not one of them is missing. Why do you complain, Jacob? Why do you say, Israel, "My way is hidden from the Lord; my cause is disregarded by my God"? Do you not know? Have you not heard? The Lord is the everlasting God, the Creator of the ends of the earth. He will not grow tired or weary, and his understanding no one can fathom.

Isaiah 40:21–23, 25–28

There is a certain amount of peace in knowing we cannot completely wrap our human minds and hearts around the depths of God. There is a certain amount of comfort in understanding that although God draws near to us and beckons us to draw near to Him, He is not completely attainable.

God remains larger.

God remains beyond our understanding and certainly beyond manageable.

Try as we may, we cannot reel Him in. We cannot "harness" Him. Not through prayer, not through worship, not through service, not in any way. When the apostle Paul bumped into this truth, he dropped everything else and started singing . . .

> Oh the depth of the riches both of the wisdom and knowledge of God! How unsearchable are His judgments and unfathomable His ways! For who has known the mind of the Lord, or who became His counselor? Or who has first given to Him that it might be paid back to him again? For from Him and through Him and to Him are all things. To Him be the glory forever. Amen.

Romans 11:33–36 NASB

There is a scene in *The Chronicles of Narnia* that plays over and over in my mind and heart. Aslan is a lion who represents Jesus. He is good, full of compassion, and he has a sweet, special relationship with the sons of Adam and the daughters of Eve (the children who find themselves in Narnia). They draw close to Him, talk with Him—and the sweet thing is that he enjoys talking with them too. One day Lucy and her sister are with Aslan when he roars a mighty, terrifying roar. One of the girls says to the other, "Aslan is not a tame lion!" To which the other responds, "No, he's not. But he is a good lion."

My friends, God is not tame—but He is good.

Melissa, when God frightens me . . . David, when He doesn't seem to make sense, I dig deep in my spiritual roots and find a shelter there. I know that you are blessed to have deep spiritual roots too....

157

Melissa, when you sing you minister to our souls, you draw us to the throne of God! You make a way for us in the wilderness, you raise up valleys and bring the mountains low. I'm not a singer, but I have a song for you. For when God responds to our prayers in the way He's responding now, there's nothing left to do but sing. In fact, we—your faith family—Melissa and David, we have a song for you. And we're going to sing it now.

> Jesus loves me, this I know.
> For the Bible tells me so.
> Little ones to Him belong . . . they are weak but He is strong.
> Yes, Jesus loves me!
> Yes, Jesus loves me.
> Yes, Jesus loves me!
> The Bible tells me so.

A New Beginning

I think it was February when David and Melissa called and invited Tom and me to lunch. They had something they wanted our spiritual counsel on. We ate at the local barbecue dive and talked about life and winter and our children. Finally David and Melissa got around to asking us their question: "What do you think about adoption?"

My heart took a happy little leap. I'm all for it! But I wanted to give Tom a chance to answer—after all, he was their spiritual leader. Tom led us through a discussion of the pros and cons of adoption, the things to consider, and the understanding that no child could ever take the place of the one they had lost. David and Melissa talked openly and freely about all these things, and then they shared with us that a pregnant woman in another state had heard their story and wanted to give them her baby. While they were not looking to adopt, this baby seemed to be landing in their laps.

To make a long story short, David and Melissa prayerfully considered the situation, and joyfully agreed to adopt this baby. They understood that their birth mother was having a baby boy. We kept a faithful prayer vigil with them throughout the weeks of waiting. Then, in April (the baby was due in May), Melissa called us and left this message on our answering machine: "Pastor Tom and Leighann, we just found out the baby is a *girl*! We're having a *girl*, not a boy!" I smiled when I heard her voice. I could almost feel Melissa's excitement and joy.

It wasn't until I was telling my mother that Melissa's baby was going to be a girl that she reminded me of the vision I'd had the day I knelt by my bed and prayed for David and Melissa. God had given me a word and He'd given me a picture. Suddenly I knew that He hadn't let us down. A few weeks later Melissa's baby girl was born. Her birth mother gave David and Melissa the greatest gift ever when they became parents to Remi Hope Radke. God did exceedingly abundantly beyond all that I could ask or imagine, just like He told me He would when I prayed for them the year before.

This was too good to miss, so my gears went into motion and I contacted Melissa.

"Melissa, you know how you and David testified last year on Father's Day? And how the entire church walked through this past year with you? Well, I was wondering if you'd be willing to keep your baby girl away from church until Father's Day this year. We'll orchestrate the entire service around how we can take God at His word and know that He answers our prayers. Then at the end, we'll recap last year's testimony (we had it on video) and show some excerpts from Elisha's memorial service. Then I want you to come up and sing the Gaither song, 'Because He Lives,' and when you get to that part about how sweet it is to hold a newborn baby, I want David to walk in with your baby girl and let us all have a *glory to God hallelujah good time!*"

Melissa and Remi Praising God

Although Melissa didn't like the idea of having to keep her baby away from us all the way until Father's

159

Day, and she wasn't that fond of what she called "that old Gaither song," I talked her into humoring me, and we had us a *glory to God hallelujah good time* on Father's Day.

Today Remi Hope Radke is six years old. She lives in Texas with her mom and dad and her little brother, Rocco.

God Is Bigger Than That

I love to tell this story because God used it in my life to show me that He will never be undone. When He gives you His word, He means to see it through. I would like to say that I marched through Melissa's journey trusting and believing and never shifting in my faith. But that wouldn't be honest. I struggled that year with "whys" and "how comes" and "for heaven's sakes!" I wept and I cried and often I felt the weight of having to somehow make excuses for God so that people's faith wouldn't be shattered. But in the end, God showed me. He showed me that He is perfectly capable of making His own name glorious and that I don't have to know what He's up to in order to rest assured He's up to something good.

Misty

A few years ago I had my own Melissa kind of experience. It has to do with another baby girl. On June 1, 2010, I lay on the floor in my daughter's empty bedroom (well, it wasn't completely empty; there were trophies and dried flowers and other trinkets scattered about as evidence of her recent teenage years), and I wailed. I couldn't cry loud enough or long enough to release the anguish in my soul. Tom lay down beside me with tears in his eyes and just listened. When my tears were spent, I lay there and wondered how God could be so cruel.

All of Mikel's life I'd prayed faithfully and fervently for her to navigate her way through growing up with the goal of finding herself in college, secure in God's direction for her life. My gorgeous daughter had just graduated from high school, had more than $76,000 of scholarships waiting for her at college, and we were almost to the place I'd dreamed we would be from the moment I heard I was pregnant. The final hurdle standing between my dreams and her achieving them was the relationship she had with her boyfriend. She and I had several discussions about him, one of which I remember well. It was the day she was headed to her junior prom, and it went something like this: "Mikel, I'm letting you go to the prom with him, but I don't want you dating him."

To which she responded, "Why not?"

"Because he doesn't love Jesus," I answered.

Being a quick-witted little chip off two communicating blocks, she quickly added (with a twinkle in her eyes), "Oh, but he *likes* Him very much."

Well, "liking Jesus very much" combined with Mikel's free will, and mine and Tom's multitude of mistakes, led to Mikel leaving us while we were out of town that summer to move into an apartment with her now boyfriend. We'd confronted the two of them the night before and had no success trying to convince either of them that there was a better way to move forward in their relationship; thus my writhing in anguish on her bedroom floor.

Over the next several weeks Tom and I spent a whole lot of time on our knees in the same spot I'd been a few years before, praying for Melissa and her baby. We begged God mostly to keep Mikel from getting pregnant. One day we were at the lake with Kaleigh and TJ—trying desperately to go on with life in some semblance of normalcy even though our hearts were shattered and our faith shaken—when Tom got a text message from a pastor friend of his who lived in the town where Mikel had moved. He asked if the rumors were true, if Mikel was pregnant and living with Austin. Tom told him that as far as we knew she was not pregnant, but that yes, they were living together, and he thanked his friend for his prayers. (You've got to love the grapevine.) A few days after that text message, we discovered the rumors were true. Our eighteen-year-old daughter was pregnant.

We were devastated. Never had I ever felt like the devil was mocking me as much as I felt it during those days. I told Tom that I didn't even want to pray because it seemed that the very things I was asking God NOT to do were being intercepted by Satan. God seemed to be sitting silent while Satan hijacked my daughter's life. Up until the summer of 2010, I had a kind of childlike trust in God, especially where my children were concerned. As I think back on it, maybe it was naïve. I prayed, and I fully realized that there were some things I could not control, but I believed that God would take care of those things. Keeping my daughter from getting pregnant at eighteen was one of those things! We gave her a promise ring, told her how sacred sex was, and taught her to wait until marriage. From before she can even remember, we told her that the second most important decision she'd make in her life would be the decision of whom to marry. She was taught the importance of marrying a man who loved the Lord and who honored and respected her and her family. I took it for granted that, since we'd done those things, God would see us through.

Throughout Mikel's first trimester of pregnancy Tom and I grieved. To me this baby represented the death of every dream I'd ever had for my precious, flesh-and-blood answer to prayer, my miracle child (as she was the baby I had after dealing with infertility). Her pregnancy was harder for me to deal with than the cancer I'd been diagnosed with in March of that same year.

Meanwhile, Mikel experienced a healthy pregnancy. During the months that she was growing a baby, she and I reconnected with each other. We shared meals together, I took her shopping, and we talked. . . . We had a lot of difficult conversations. Tom and I prayed, we cried, and we tried our best to lead our church with our broken hearts. People were wonderful to us. They shared their stories and promised us that things would be different in time.

Much of what I'm writing in this book came out of what I learned during those days.

On February 9, 2011, Misty Sierra Crowe was born. She looked just like my daughter, and even more like her sister Kaleigh, all ten pounds and two ounces of her. (Kaleigh was nine pounds, ten ounces at birth.) Mikel did fine, although she'd gained seventy pounds during her pregnancy and had a C-section. And her boyfriend, Austin, stood faithfully by her side every minute of the two days she spent in labor. I'll never forget watching the tears streaming down his cheeks as he stood over his daughter's little bucket in the newborn nursery. There is truly something miraculous and marvelous about the birth of babies.

I loved Misty from the moment I first laid eyes on her. During the first year of her interesting life I got to feed her lots of bottles and change lots of diapers. She and I quickly became special friends. When she was still small enough to be carried in an infant seat, Mikel would bring her into our house and her toes would stretch and her face light up with a smile, while her arms reached toward me—she greeted me with her entire being. I spent hours rocking her in the room where I'd begged God not to create her. And I held her in my arms, felt her sweet head nestle close to mine, and wondered at how I could have ever known what an amazing blessing she was going to be.

She's nineteen months old as I write this. My cancer has come back and I'm going through chemo treatments. The first week I had chemo, Mikel brought Misty to see me. It was the day after my worst day (thankfully I'm only having one worst day each round of treatment). I was weak and I'm sure not looking my best. Misty crawled into my lap, smiled at me, and then laid her head on my shoulder. I looked across the room at Mikel and said, "Oh, Mikel, Misty is the best medicine ever." Then I confessed, "If it were just you, Kaleigh, TJ, and Dad, I'm not sure I'd even want to go through this treatment. But for Misty, I'll do it. I'm a good Nana and I want to be in her life for a whole lot of years to come."

Mikel was a bit miffed that I wouldn't be willing to suffer for them, but then she smiled and said, "I knew there was a reason for Misty!" And we both smiled because in the midst of all our mistakes and messes—things we wish we could do over so that we might have been able to avoid the hurt of the past few years—we also realized that God is bigger than all that. He alone knew that Misty would be a blessing, and He brought her to us at just the right time.

Me and Misty

God Is Bigger Than . . .

This has been a very long chapter. But I wanted to tell you these stories so that you could know how I learned to trust God through some of the most difficult days of my faith. I'm grateful to Melissa and Mikel for letting me tell you these things. Both of them are strong, beautiful women who have great stories to tell and ministries to fulfill.

I don't know what your story might be. I don't know if you are writhing in agony on a bedroom floor, weeping in the parking lot of a doctor's office, or soaking in your tub and having a heart-to-heart with Jesus. (Believe me, I've had some of those!) Wherever you are, no matter what you are facing, I want you to know that God is bigger than whatever it is. He does work all things together for good, and if it's not good just yet, it's because He's still working.

Treasure Hunt

Personal Reflection

- Have you ever had a "God is bigger than that" kind of experience in your life? If so, what did you learn about God? What did you learn about yourself? What did you learn about life?

Discussion Questions

1. Share your "God is bigger than that" experiences and the things you learned from them.
2. If someone in your group is going through their "God is bigger than that" experience right now, encourage her and pray for her.

Treasure Verse

Do you not know? Have you not heard? The Lord is the everlasting God, the Creator of the ends of the earth. He will not grow tired or weary, and his understanding no one can fathom. He gives strength to the weary and increases the power of the weak.

Isaiah 40:28–29

12

Let God Define Good

And we know that God causes all things to work together for good
to those who love God, to those who are called according to His
purpose.

Romans 8:28 NASB

I once heard a friend speak on the parable of the wheat and tares
(Matthew 13:24–30). In this parable, Jesus told about a farmer
who planted good wheat seed in his field. Then at night his enemies
came and littered his field with weed seed (tares). When the crop
began to grow, the farmer's workers saw the weeds and suggested
to the farmer that they remove them immediately. But the farmer
told them to leave the weeds alone lest they damage the wheat in
the process of weeding the field. So the weeds and the wheat were
left alone to grow together until the harvest. Kate gave several
personal illustrations of "tares" that she'd observed in her life.
She confessed that she longed for God to remove those "tares,"
but instead He allowed them to stay. Then, after some time, she
grew to understand that some of those "tares" were wheat after all.

I've never forgotten Kate's message. She was encouraging us
to let God define good. Our understanding is limited. Sometimes

our affections are misplaced. Certainly our perspective is different from God's. Therefore, He alone knows what is and is not "good" for us.

"Never, Lord! This Shall Never Happen to You"

One of the best examples of a passionate believer who was severely mistaken in his estimation of what was good and what was not is an encounter Jesus had with Peter. This intimate and most likely embarrassing altercation between Jesus and Peter took place not long after Peter's great confession of Christ as the Son of the living God. (See Matthew 16:13–20.) Not only did Jesus applaud Peter for his confession, but He also assured His disciple that God alone had revealed this truth to him. Then Jesus went on to tell Peter that the very keys of the kingdom of heaven would be entrusted to him, he would be instrumental in the building of the church, and the gates of hell could not prevail against him.

As I read those verses I'm prompted to wonder if the anointing of spiritual authority and power that Jesus bestowed on Peter awakened the powers of darkness to take notice of Peter and target him for attack. For after that moment in time, Peter encountered some amazing trials—and experienced some devastating defeat in his walk with the Lord. The first of these incidents happened soon thereafter.

Scripture records that after Jesus blessed Peter with that powerful promise, He began to explain to Peter and the rest of His disciples the details regarding His upcoming death and resurrection.

> From that time on Jesus began to explain to his disciples that he must go to Jerusalem and suffer many things at the hands of the elders, chief priests and teachers of the law, and that he must be killed and on the third day be raised to life.
>
> Matthew 16:21

I would imagine that Peter felt more comfortable in his relationship with Jesus after Jesus gave him those accolades as a result of his powerful profession of faith. Most likely Peter was a natural-born leader and was accustomed to speaking his mind no matter the situation. He was certainly impulsive in his behavior (as demonstrated the night he stepped out of a perfectly good boat into a raging sea). So given his growing confidence as a leader amongst Jesus' disciples, Peter took it upon himself to pull Jesus off to the side and rebuke Him. Take a minute and reread that sentence. Peter took Jesus off to the side and *rebuked* Him. That is some true grit! (Read it for yourself in both Matthew 16:22 and Mark 8:32.)

> "Never, Lord!" he said, "This shall never happen to you!"
>
> Matthew 16:22

What brass! What fortitude! What a mistake! My cheeks are growing warm with humiliation for him as I write this. Rather than correct Peter privately, or even applaud his affectionate concern, Jesus turned to make sure the other disciples were close enough to hear Him, and He reprimanded Peter soundly:

> Get behind me, Satan! You are a stumbling block to me; you do not have in mind the things of God, but the things of men.
>
> Matthew 16:23

Mark recorded much the same words (see Mark 8:33). In Peter's definition of good, Jesus could not go to Jerusalem; be rejected by the elders, chief priests, and teachers of the law; and be killed and after three days rise again. In Peter's mind and heart, that was not good. No matter what, he could not let that happen, not to Jesus, not on his watch. But we know that what Jesus was about to do was the ultimate good that had been His destiny from the foundation of the world (see Ephesians 1:3–10). We know this because we live on the other side of Jesus' life, death, resurrection, and ascension to the right hand of God, where He rules and reigns today. Romans 8:28 has been completed in Jesus.

But Peter wasn't where we are. He was on the other side of Romans 8:28. He was on the other side of Jesus' suffering: the mocking, the plucking of His beard, spitting in His face, thorn-pierced brow, and severe beating of the scourge. How could all of that be *good*? Death on the cross? Crosses were not covered with gold and inlaid with diamonds; they were symbols of Rome's most tortuous punishment reserved for the worst criminals! From Peter's perspective none of this was good.

What Do You Have in Mind?

Can't you understand why Peter felt the way he did? Have you been there too? I have a friend whose son committed suicide; what part of Romans 8:28 will meet her there? I have another whose husband's addiction to alcohol is robbing her of the family she dreamed of having, and another whose husband and son are fighting advanced stages of cancer. Where is the good in all of that?!

Jesus' response tells us where we have to go in order to expand our definition of good. In His words He reveals a mystery to us. That mystery is that God is able to create endless new meanings of the word *good*.

Jesus was not driven by a need to humiliate Peter. He didn't rebuke him in front of His other disciples to tear him down so that later He could build him up. Rather, Jesus wanted all of His disciples to learn the lesson I'm about to share with you. Take another look at Jesus' rebuke:

> "Get behind me, Satan!" he said. "You do not have in mind the concerns of God, but merely human concerns."
>
> Mark 8:33

Jesus told Peter that he was mistaken in his definition of good because he did not have God at the center of his mind. Peter had the things of this world as the source of his thinking and most likely his feeling. Peter didn't know what was good because he didn't have in mind the things of God. Peter was still trapped in limited, sin-stained, misdirected, stinkin' thinkin. His problem was the same problem Eve had when the serpent challenged her to entertain the possibility that God was something other than good (see Genesis 3:1–7). Peter's mind was set on the things of men; the things of this world; the things that have been distorted, tainted, spoiled, and ruined by sin.

When we have the things of this world in the center of our hearts and our minds, we are deceived into thinking certain things are good and other things are not good. And while our understanding makes perfect sense to us, anytime those definitions of good lead us to question the goodness, the wisdom, the power, or the love of God, then we are mistaken. God is good; what He does is good. He never has been and never will be anything less than good to us. But His good and ours might often be two very different things.

What might happen if we let God define good?

We Take Captive Every Thought

In his second letter to the church at Corinth, Paul urged believers to be diligent in training their minds to be one with the mind of God. As women who long to hear the voice of God, we will hear Him all the more when our minds and His are filled with the same thoughts. Paul urged the Corinthian believers to approach this task (of having the mind of Christ) like warfare.

> For though we live in the world, we do not wage war as the world does. The weapons we fight with are not the weapons of the world. On the contrary, they have divine power to demolish strongholds. We demolish arguments and every pretension that sets itself up

against the knowledge of God, and we take captive every thought to make it obedient to Christ.

2 Corinthians 10:3–5

Sometimes I think we tend to be wimpy. We expect our Christian lives to be easy, and when they're not we get mad or we pout or we wonder where our faith faltered, or worse, where God let us down. Can I have a witness? In these verses Paul tells us that as long as we live in the world, we are engaged in battle. This world, all of it, is a spiritual battlefield. That's the news. It's neither good nor bad; it's just the way it is.

The good news is that we have superpower weapons! Our weapons are empowered by God to demolish strongholds. What are strongholds? Strongholds are the things that we believe that do not line up with the mind of God! They are the deceptions and the lies and the superficial, the temporal, and the wood, hay, and stubble that will burn up in the end. Strongholds are the things of this world that blind us to the things of God. They are the wicked web woven by the prince of the darkness to render us captive to his limited power and evil ways. Strongholds are strong, but they are not too strong!

Strongholds are demolished by the weapons we have! So what are these weapons that have power to demolish arguments and every pretension that sets itself up against the knowledge of God? The weapons we have are prayer and God's Word!

Because Jesus paid sin's price, He set us free from sin's power. When we asked Jesus to forgive us of our sins, when we accepted His death on the cross as the payment for our sin, and when we chose to believe that God raised Him from the dead, proving His power over sin and death, then we were made as righteous as Christ in the eyes of God. Therefore, God urges us to draw near to His powerful, unmatched throne of grace, where we have audience with the King of Glory and find all that we need to live our lives in victory and not defeat (Hebrews 10:19–23). Prayer is a weapon that has power to demolish strongholds and every argument and pretension that sets itself up against the knowledge of God.

God's Word is our other weapon.

> The word of God is alive and active. Sharper than any double-edged sword, it penetrates even to dividing soul and spirit, joints and marrow; it judges the thoughts and attitudes of the heart.
>
> Hebrews 4:12

When your definition of good is disrupted by what seems to be bad, let God's Word have the final say. God always tells you the truth in His Word. Unlike the devil, who prowls about looking for an opportunity to devour you (2 Peter 5:8), God is up-front and honest with you. He loves you, longs to make himself known to you, and stands ready to demonstrate His power and His love in and through you. You learn to trust God's Word as you choose to live obedient to God's Word. The power of God's Word is *not* released in the lives of people who give only lip service to God. Those who are not serious about walking in obedience to Christ are fooling themselves if they think they have power of any kind.

But for you, because you are a woman eager to hear and follow hard after the voice of God, with prayer and the Word of God you have power to demolish strongholds, arguments, and every pretension that sets itself up against the knowledge of God. With prayer and the Word of God you have the ability to take captive every thought (and perception of what is and is not good) and make it bow down to the lordship of Christ.

There Was More to Jesus' Rebuke of Peter

Before we bring this chapter to a close, I want to take you back to Mark 8. Jesus rebuked Peter in front of His disciples because they all needed to be forewarned that a mind that is divided between the things of this world and the things of God is a mind that will misunderstand the voice of God. But after He chastised Peter, Jesus then called the crowd to listen and shared a bit more.

> Then he called the crowd to him along with his disciples and said: "Whoever wants to be my disciple must deny themselves and take up their cross and follow me. For whoever wants to save their life will lose it, but whoever loses their life for me and for the gospel will save it. What good is it for someone to gain the whole world, yet forfeit their soul?"
>
> Mark 8:34–36

See, I told you that God's Word always tells you the truth. God does not lie, He is honest, and He is clear. His voice is not muffled. Jesus used this teachable moment to further expound on the requirement necessary to hear, understand, and follow His voice. In order to have your mind on the things of God, you must also have your heart set on the things of God. And in order to have your heart set on the things of God, you must deny yourself, take up your cross, and follow Jesus.

In other words, you (and I) must consider our very lives—the only lives we know, the ones we are living on this earth—as nothing compared to the life that is to come. The soul that is housed in the human body is far more valuable (because it is far more lasting) than the body that houses it. My son told me a long time ago that when he dies his bones are going to stay in the ground but that he is going to heaven to live with God. And TJ was absolutely right. The only things that really matter are those things that will last forever, and the only things lasting—on this earth today—are the souls of people.

When our affections, our passions, our dreams, goals, desires, and ambitions land on the here and now, then our affections, our passions, our dreams, goals, desires, and ambitions fall far short of the glory of God. Unless you and I are willing to deny ourselves (and all that comes so naturally to our earthly existence), take up our crosses (those terrible things that we would never consider "good"), and follow Christ (refusing to consider Him anything other than loving and kind), we will miss Him. When we allow God to define what is and is not good in our lives, we are learning to take up our crosses and follow Him.

Application for Me

Cancer isn't good; it's terrible. Surgery, scans, scopes, doctors' visits, chemotherapy, ugh! Cancer isn't something God ordained. It's a terrible by-product of sin. But when my cancer returned I was forced to face my mortality. I always knew I would die *some* day, but with cancer in my liver I was faced with the very real possibility that my day might come sooner than I thought. I was surprised at how much I hated the thought of death. I wanted to be like Paul and be able to gladly proclaim that to live is Christ and to die is gain (Philippians 1:21), but for me to live is holding my granddaughter and seeing my other two children married (someday). It's welcoming more grandchildren into this world and writing books and loving my husband. To live is loving the people at Thompson Station Church, and speaking at women's retreats, and spending time at my "laughing place" in the beautiful North Carolina mountains, and taking that trip to Europe that Tom and I have talked about for years. To live *here* seems so much better than death.

I know that God understands me. He knows what it's like to be human. After all, Jesus even asked that the cup of suffering and death be exchanged for another, and He sweat great big drops of blood when He prayed. Please don't get me wrong. I am grateful for the home that will be ours forever on the other side of death, and I look forward to laughing with you over all the hubbub we made over death when we get there. But I would rather take that journey at a ripe old age full of years, like Job (Job 42:16).

So for me, my recurrence of cancer was not good. However, I know that God is good and that because God rules supreme in my life, He alone has say-so on what is allowed to invade my body.

Therefore I lay my fear and dread at the foot of the cross, where I know that God's passion for me is illustrated completely. And during those days when I didn't know if I was living or dying, I heard God say, "This cancer is purposeful. If you knew now what I'm going to do through you, you would gladly agree to have it."

Now, I don't know about you, but I've got some desperate heart cries lying at God's throne of grace. There are several things that I am waiting for Him to do. And some of the ways that God is working on those things are baffling me already. If God is going to use my suffering with cancer to do something good, then I am eager to submit to His wisdom, His power, and His love, and trust Him to do exactly what He has set out to do.

Along the way God also reminded me of a quiet time I had one evening when I was serving as a summer missionary in rural Nevada. I sat under the setting sun and made Him a promise. I told God that I wanted to give my entire life to serve Him. I trusted Him, believed He had the very best plans for my life, and wanted to walk in them. I gave Him my honest desire for a husband, for children, for a career that was significant, and as much as I was able, I committed all of me to all of Him. When my cancer returned a few months ago, God reminded me of that promise. Gently He said, "I didn't have to ask if it was okay with you to have to deal with cancer again. I knew it would be fine. You told me already, a long time ago, that you trusted me with your life."

I don't like going through chemotherapy. It stinks. But I do like knowing that God is up to something good. I'm not sure what it is just yet, but I am resting now in the knowledge that even if I'm sick next week when I go for number three of twelve treatments, God is working and He is answering and He is keeping His word to me.

You may be going through something far worse than chemo treatments. Or it may not be quite as bad. I don't know what you're dealing with, but I know God, and I know that He's good, and I know that He will work whatever it is into good for you. Just let Him define the good.

Treasure Hunt

Personal Reflections

- Read Matthew 16:13–27. Imagine what it might have been like to have been Peter.
- How would you have felt if Jesus had rebuked you in front of His other disciples?
- What part of Jesus' command to
  - deny yourself
  - take up your cross
  - follow Him

  is hardest for you to do?

Discussion Questions

1. Has God ever redefined good in your life? If so, share with your group how He did that.
2. Share which parts of living here and now are hardest to let go.
3. Was there a time in your life when you gave God everything? How long ago was that? How does the memory of that experience impact your relationship with God today?

Treasure Verse

Then Jesus said to his disciples, "Whoever wants to be my disciple must deny themselves and take up their cross and follow me. For whoever wants to save their life will lose it, but whoever loses their life for me will find it."

Matthew 16:24–25

PART FOUR

God Will Make a Way

God is making a way in your desert. Streams are springing up in your wasteland. Do you not perceive it? My dear sister in Christ, the day will come (maybe sooner than you think) when this desert will be no more. You will break forth in singing, and the sorrow that lasted for the night will be transformed into JOY in the morning!

> We all have desert seasons in God when everything in our spiritual life is dry, dusty, and void of inspiration. The only way through is to make a decision in advance that no matter how tough the slogging gets, we're never going to give up on our pursuit of God. We're going to abide in Christ no matter what. I'll let you in on a secret: This kind of tenacious commitment to endurance will open the path to the most meaningful dimensions of relationship with the Lord.
>
> —Bob Sorge[1]

1. Bob Sorge, *Secrets of the Secret Place* (Kansas City, MO: Oasis House, 2001), 121.

13

God Will Make a Way

Forget the former things; do not dwell on the past. See, I am doing a new thing! Now it springs up; do you not perceive it? I am making a way in the wilderness and streams in the wasteland.

Isaiah 43:18–19

Most of our efforts to hear God's voice center around needing to know that we are safe, that our troubles will not last forever, or that our lives have some sort of meaning and purpose. We long to fulfill the plans God has for us. We desperately cry out to Him so we can know that He is going to see us through the difficult things that come our way. And we scurry about, searching for significance as we discover the difference between a mind set on the things of this world and a mind that shares the thoughts of God.

God created us to need Him. He created in us a hard drive to want to serve Him. Many people live their lives ignorant of these facts. But you are not one of those. You are reading this book because you want to know God. You want to walk in constant communication with Him. You want your life to complete the "good works" He had in mind for you when He created you in your mother's womb (see Ephesians 2:8–10). So as you continue in your quest for understanding how to hear the voice of God, consider Isaiah and the promise God gave him to give to us.

> Forget the former things; do not dwell on the past. I am doing a new thing! Now it springs up; do you not perceive it? I am making a way in the wilderness and streams in the wasteland.

Isaiah 43:18–19

God is making a way for you to hear Him, to walk with Him, and to experience Him work new things in and through your life. Most likely God has allowed the difficult circumstances you are facing today to draw you near to Him so that He can accomplish these new things in your midst. Don't be blinded by your troubles. If your life seems more like a desert wasteland than a fertile valley, then this chapter is for you.

Desert Defined

God literally called me to full-time vocational ministry while I was in the deserts of rural Nevada. I briefly mentioned in the last chapter that I spent a summer in Nevada as a student missionary. I was assigned to serve in Mina, Gabbs, and Middlegate, Nevada. The people who lived and worked in these towns called their "metropolitan" ministry MGM. This was meant to be funny because the combined population of Mina, Gabbs, and Middlegate might have been equal to the number of students who attended my high school!

The day I left home to travel to Nevada was the first time I'd ever flown. I flew on an American Airlines flight in a window seat not far from the back of the plane, where smoking was still allowed. But even the smoke didn't bother me too much as I took in the wonder of seeing the world from that lofty perspective. That day I fell in love with flying; it did and does remind me that there is always another point of view on the world.

My summer assignment was, up to that time, the most difficult experience I'd ever had in my life. I signed up to be a summer missionary with the hopes of being assigned to Hawaii or Hollywood, California, or even New York City. But, alas, I was deposited in Mina, Nevada (the middle one of the three towns that made up MGM), with a missionary couple who lived in a single-wide trailer. Half of their single wide was converted into worship space, and the other half housed them, their two sons, and six yappy dogs. I slept on the fold-out sofa in their living room. For four weeks of my ten-week commitment I lived with this missionary couple. They'd recently adopted two boys who'd been taken from an abusive home. The dynamics in our half of that single wide were interesting to say the least.

But that's not the part of my summer missions experience that I want to talk with you about. The part I remember most was living in the desert. I'd never been anywhere with no trees, but in rural Nevada you could drive for miles and miles and see only rugged hills scattered with sagebrush, an occasional herd of wild mustangs, and jackrabbits. Nevada's rabbits were nothing like the fuzzy bunnies we had in Georgia. Their rabbits reminded me of Bugs Bunny, only they weren't as clever at staying alive. They littered the roads even more than possums and armadillos do in Tennessee. The only landmark on my scenic drive to my mission assignment was the infamous Area 51. This was barren land!

When I discovered that my assignment was in rural Nevada, I anticipated a summer full of sunshine—after all, I was going to live in the desert! (I was going through my "suntan Barbie" phase in life.) Unfortunately, it turned out to be the rainiest summer ever for rural Nevada. But for me it was an adventure. I was going to a place I'd never been before, and I immediately fell in love with the great big sky and the wide-open space.

The prophet Isaiah spoke to the children of Israel while they were living in a desert too. Only theirs was not merely a physical desert but a spiritual one as well. I love the word pictures used in Scripture to describe spiritual realities in our lives. The spiritual desert the Israelites were facing, the one that Isaiah was addressing, is described in the first eight verses of Isaiah 43. Here are some of the words that he used: blazing fires and flooded rivers (v. 2); children scattered to the four corners of the earth (vv. 5–6); eyes that are blind and ears that are deaf (v. 8).

Have you ever lived in deserts such as these? Does your heart burn with anger, resentment, and fury? I have a friend whose husband left her for another woman. Although she prayed for years that he would recognize the error of his ways and return to her, he remains with that woman. Now my friend struggles to live with the relationship her children are developing with the woman who, in her mind and heart, ripped her family to shreds. That, my friends, is a blazing fire.

Do you feel like you're wading through flood waters when you get out of bed in the morning? Flood waters are rancid and they leave rot in their wake. I never knew what it was like to be sick until now. During the week of my chemo treatments, I walk around for three days listening to the pump pouring fluid in me that is killing cancer cells, but along with those, it is killing my healthy cells too. I know that when that pump comes off, I am going to be smacked down, wiped out, nauseated, and sluggish. On the fourth through seventh days of treatment I am wading in what feels like flood waters. Perhaps you have felt that way too.

Are you a mother who knows what it's like to have your children scattered to the four corners of the earth? I've learned in the past few years that having even one of my children living in a culture I never wanted her to experience is worse than having her on the other side of the world serving as a missionary! To have your children separated from your heart is perhaps the most desperate desert of all.

Blind eyes and deaf ears . . . who can even begin to describe the frustration of being in the dark and hearing nothing but silence? Or what if the blind eyes and deaf ears belong to those you love? How agonizing it is to watch them bump into obstacles that leave them battered and bruised, obstacles they could have easily avoided if they could just see what you see and hear what you hear! Certainly Isaiah did a very good job of describing the desert experiences of our lives.

The deserts we find ourselves in today exist for three reasons:

1. We live in a sin-stained world.

Sometimes people say to me, "I can never believe in a God who would allow such suffering in the world." This is what I .tell them: "Although this is the world God made, in its present state it is a *sick* shadow that barely resembles what our loving Creator had in mind when He called it 'very good.' God is as appalled at the suffering in this world as you are. In fact, He couldn't stand idly by and watch the people He created suffer forever. That's why He sent His Son to die."

When you find yourself in a desert, you are sometimes there because you live in a sin-stained world.

2. We experience the effects of the mistakes of others.

Because we are not independent creatures but interdependent creation, and because God made us in His very own image, we are prone to love one another. Love is a strong emotion that is as real in hurt, pain, and suffering as it is in joy, happiness, and prosperity. You may be living in a desert today that was created by the poor choices of someone you love very much.

3. We make poor choices ourselves.

Sometimes our desert experiences are nobody's fault but our own. This was often the case with God's beloved children of Israel. In fact, this is the cause of the desert experience they are having in Isaiah 43.

A desert is a difficult place to be. Deserts come in many shapes and sizes, but they all have in common a sense of barrenness and desperate hunger for the voice of God.

Consider the Cactus

The cactus is not exactly a plant that is exchanged between lovers. In fact, the cactus plant is quite prickly and not very pretty (unless of course you like that kind of thing). I learned this about cacti—the most prominent desert plants: they developed spines in order to protect themselves from their harsh environments.

One thing I learned about living in the desert: If you're not careful, you can become a cactus. Because I want to conserve what sanity I have and survive in the hot environment, I tend to develop spines, and if people get too close to me, I might be a bit prickly. Be careful not to become a prickly cactus just because you are experiencing life in the desert.

What is your desert? Take an honest look around you. Describe the circumstances that stand between you and the experience of God's abundant blessing in your life. What is it that is making your life hard? What is keeping you from hearing the voice of God?

Once you have the definition of your desert in mind, I want you to say this aloud: "God will make a way in my desert."

Desert Designed

What would you say if I told you that God actually allowed this desert in your life because His perfect love chose it for you? If you said that to me, I might say, "You gotta be kiddin' me! Not *this* desert. This particular desert is evil to the core. It's designed to destroy me, and there is *no way* that it could ever have been allowed by the kind, tender, and loving heart of God!"

That's what *I* would say . . . but let's look at what God would say. . . .

Your desert is designed to test your faith and develop perseverance.

Consider it pure joy, my brothers, whenever you face trials of many kinds, *because you know that the testing of your faith develops perseverance.* Let perseverance finish its work so that you may be mature and complete, not lacking anything.

James 1:2–4

James really did say to consider your desert "pure joy." Now, I've experienced joy—it is often wrapped in pretty paper and tied with a bow. It comes early on Christmas morning with the smells of hot cocoa and sausage biscuits. The joy that I like carries a sense of anticipation and excitement. There's laughter and loved ones with me when I experience joy.

But James said that as a child of God, I can experience "pure joy" whenever I face "trials of many kinds." Uh . . . joy? Maybe not "joy" but "pure joy." There must be something very different about pure joy and the kind of joy I've described. *Pure joy* comes directly from heaven wrapped in "trials of many kinds." And it is good for me because it tests my faith and develops perseverance.

The Christmas morning kind of joy is fleeting. Sometimes it can be gone by 4 p.m. on Christmas afternoon. In my family, we've had Christmas days when we were moping about by four o'clock. Somebody had already done somebody wrong and we were all kinds of miffed about it. But the kind of joy that James is describing is not fleeting. It lasts, and it finishes its work. That's why it's called *pure.*

Can you praise God for the desert you're in now that you know it is designed to give you *pure joy?*

Your desert is designed to discipline you.

Endure hardship as discipline; God is treating you as his children. For what children are not disciplined by their father? If you are not disciplined—and everyone undergoes discipline—then you are not legitimate, not true sons and daughters at all. Moreover, we have all had human fathers who disciplined us and we respected them for it. How much more should we submit to the Father of spirits and live! They disciplined us for a little while as they thought best;

but God disciplines us for our good, in order that we may share in his holiness. No discipline seems pleasant at the time, but painful. Later on, however, it produces a harvest of righteousness and peace for those who have been trained by it.

Hebrews 12:7–11

There is not much I love about these particular verses, but there is one thing. At least the writer of Hebrews understood that *hardship* has to be *endured*. That's a whole lot easier for me to comprehend than James's "pure joy."

"Endure hardship as discipline; God is treating you as his children." I have worked with children much of my life. I've directed summer camps, led children's ministries in churches, and taught countless others how to do the same. But there are only three children who were mine (and my husband's) to discipline: Mikel, Kaleigh, and TJ. Those three were my responsibility. Their behavior was mine to shape. Their thought processes were mine to influence. Their choices were mine to critique. Now, there were plenty of times when they weren't happy with my discipline. And there were lots of times when they felt like I had no right to tell them what to do. In fact, I can't think of a single time that any one of them thanked me for a spanking or a time-out. But the right to discipline my three was given to me because I birthed them into this world. I never expected them to *like* what I was doing when I was correcting them.

Every time my discipline was "endured" by my children, I suffered their backlash because my love for them is vigilant, fierce, and ferocious. More than anything in the world I want my children to succeed, to be all that God intended them to be, and to be fulfilled in their own lives. I want them to know true joy, experience deep peace, and live lives of significance. These desires are at the core of the deepest longings of my heart. They pull on me day and night. I am driven by my violent love for my children.

God is a perfect Father. All of those things that I feel for my three, God experiences for you. Only He feels them more and better.

Think of God's discipline in the same way that you think of yours (if you are a mother). Some of the hardship you are enduring is coming your way because your Father is focused on shaping and molding you into the image He had for you when He created you. God is intent on seeing you become the woman He longs for you to be . . . successful, fulfilled, full of joy, overflowing with peace, and living a life of powerful significance.

Now, if that is the goal—if that is the prize—isn't the hardship you are currently enduring perhaps worth the present pain?

Your desert is designed to allow you to experience deeper intimacy with God.

For I am convinced that neither death nor life, neither angels nor demons, neither the present nor the future, not any powers, neither height nor depth, *nor anything else in all creation, will be able to separate us from the love of God that is in Christ Jesus our Lord.*

Romans 8:38–39

This is perhaps the greatest part of being in the desert. When hardship and trials of many kinds come your way, God promises to walk with you so close that you can almost hear His heartbeat. But in order to experience the presence of God in your desert, you have to take time to rest.

My chemo has taught me how to rest. Resting is releasing the thoughts that try desperately to make sense of your predicament and search frantically for a way of escape. Resting is taking time to sit still and look around. Let me see if I can explain this. One fall afternoon I took Misty to the backyard and together we sat under our willow tree. She'd never been under our willow tree. I lay on my back, looked up into the blue October sky, and watched her as she danced with the willow branches that embraced her. I wasn't writing a book. . . . I wasn't wondering how long I'll live on earth. . . . I wasn't worried over my son-in-law who was soon to deploy to Afghanistan. . . . For those few minutes, Misty and I were resting in God's arms and dancing in the willow's branches.

Another morning I had my quiet time on the patio. It had been unseasonably warm for October in Tennessee, and Misty loves the outdoors. So dressed in her footy pajamas, she explored the backyard while I sat at the table and read my Bible. Right in the middle of reading, I looked up and was struck by the beauty of my own backyard at the peak of autumn's wonder. The mums surrounding my pool were putting on a glorious show; my neighbor's red barn seemed to come right out of a picture with the blue sky behind it and the brilliant orange tree in front. For a moment I was caught up in the wonder that even in the middle of chemo treatment I get to interact with the God who made all of this!

No matter what desert you find yourself in, know this: God is in that desert with you. Experience His presence while you are there. These three truths are not truths that Paul, James, and the writer of Hebrews discovered on the mountaintops. These are truths they discovered in the desert. I am certain you will discover truths in your desert too.

My daughter Kaleigh came over to my "laughing place" (a farmhouse in the North Carolina mountains) to see me one night. She had just started her sophomore year at the University of Tennessee in Knoxville. As she and I talked, she started giving me a rare glimpse into her struggle with my cancer. She and her siblings have been strangely quiet about their own struggles, not wanting to stress me in mine. But that night Kaleigh let her guard down. She told me that as she talked with a friend, her friend explained to her that even though I am not dying, and my cancer is most likely not going to kill me, that doesn't change the fact that Kaleigh's having to deal with it. He also told her not to add to her pain by feeling guilty just because some people are sicker than her mother. He said that no matter what others were dealing with, that didn't make her situation any easier.

He then pointed out a beautiful truth. He said that because I had cancer, she was (and had been) learning to say, "My mom has cancer, praise God." He went on to explain that she wasn't praising God *for* my cancer, but she was learning to praise God *in spite of* my cancer. I told her that he was a wise friend, for in my cancer I am learning the same truth. I have cancer and I choose to praise God. She and I have learned to do that because of the desert we've found ourselves in.

Now, let me remind you that I am not saying God created your desert. But in His sovereignty He didn't rescue you from it. You are in this desert either because you made mistakes, because somebody you love made mistakes, or because you got jerked out to sea in the riptide of our world gone wrong. *But God,* in His infinite wisdom and perfect love, allowed this desert for you. Think about that for a moment.

God, in His infinite wisdom and perfect love, allowed this desert for you.

And because you are in *this* desert today, you can know that God is making a way for you in it. He will see to it that even in this particular (and maybe peculiar) desert experience, precious flowers will begin to grow. And as those flowers begin to spring up in your desert, they will release a beautiful fragrance in your life. For God is doing a new thing. Do you not perceive it?

I wrote this statement in my book *Spiritual Warfare for Women:*

Every attack from the Enemy [And by the way, many of our deserts are craftily created by the rattlesnake himself—full of scorpions and gila monsters (giant lizards) and all kinds of things that are out to get you. But nevertheless, Every attack from the Enemy] *brings with it a divine invitation from the sovereign hand of God to learn by experience what love does.*[1]

If you are living in a desert today, take courage, for God has invited you to an intimate place with Him. There are depths of His

1. Leighann McCoy, *Spiritual Warfare for Women* (Minneapolis: Bethany House Publishers, 2011), 39.

love that can only be discovered in the deserts of life. What does Isaiah tell us? Right here in these deserts, God is . . .

> . . . doing a new thing! *Now* it springs up; do you not perceive it? [He] is making a way . . . and [He is creating] springs in the wasteland.
>
> Isaiah 43:19

Now, wouldn't you imagine that the God of the desert is perfectly capable of creating streams of water right there?

That summer I spent in Nevada it rained . . . a lot! My tan faded and I discovered what happens in a desert when the rain comes. First there were little rivulets all over that desert. The water seemed to run everywhere because the ground was so hard it couldn't soak it up. But then, after so much rain continued to fall, the desert began to bloom with amazing flowers. That's right; I was surrounded by a bloomin' desert!

Maybe you feel like you've been living in a barren land and every day the storm clouds loom overhead, the rain never ceases to fall, and your hopes have grown damp and dull. I hope that you understand now that your desert is designed to bring you into a closer, more intimate relationship with your Lord, who loves you. Think of what God is showing you in your desert. Thank Him for showing you those things. Now say aloud, "God is making a way in this desert."

Desert Deserted

When streams start flowing, things start growing, and when things start growing, the desert is transformed into a beautiful garden! Don't forget that God's original intent was that you and I would live in a *garden* not a *desert*!

I love the classic devotional book *Streams in the Desert*. I've quoted from it often because it is so full of truths that quench my parched throat as I stumble forward in my desert. On August 1 I read this prayer:

> Dear friend, you can trust the Man who died for you. You can trust Him to thwart each plan that should be stopped and to complete each one that results in His greatest glory and your highest good. You can trust Him to lead you down the path that is the very best in this world for you.[2]

God is making a way in your desert. Streams are springing up in your wasteland. Do you not perceive it? My dear sister in Christ, the day will come (maybe sooner than you think) when this desert will be no more. You will break forth in singing, and the sorrow that lasted for the night will be transformed into *joy* in the morning! Your desert *will not last forever.*

Peter was one of Jesus' very best friends. Peter was the one that Jesus chose to replace Him as the leader of the disciples when He left to sit at the right hand of His Father. I would dare say that Peter and John were closer to Jesus when He walked on earth than anyone. No one else could possibly know the truth I'm about to share with you better than Peter. This is what Peter wants you to know:

> And the God of all grace, who called you to His eternal glory in Christ, after you have suffered a little while, will himself restore you and make you strong, firm and steadfast.
>
> 1 Peter 5:10

Your desert is not forever. In just a little while, God *himself* will restore you and make you strong, firm, and steadfast.

There is a scene in the movie *The Help* that I especially like. *The Help* tells the story of a group of African American house servants who lived in Mississippi in the 1950s. In the movie an ambitious young white journalist convinced these women ("the help") to

---

2. L. B. Cowman, ed. Jim Reimann, *Streams in the Desert* (Grand Rapids, MI: Zondervan, 1997), 295.

tell their stories. This young journalist published their stories in a book that exposed the wickedness of prejudice that prevailed in the Deep South. One of the scenes in the movie that I liked best was when Aibileen ("the help" for a young white family) pulls little Mae (the preschool daughter in the family she works for) into her lap, puts her hands on her cheeks, peers into her eyes, and speaks these words as little Mae repeats them after her: "I is kind, I is smart, and I is important."

I was taken aback by the love that beautiful, mistreated black woman had for that innocent little white girl. But my friends, the day will come when our Lord, who loves us so much, is going to lead us right out of these deserts we've found ourselves in. He's going to put His nail-scarred hands on our tear-stained cheeks, He's going to penetrate us with His compassionate gaze and speak these words—as we repeat them with Him . . . "I is strong, I is firm, and I is steadfast."

God will make a way.

Treasure Hunt

Personal Reflections

- Think of the desert you find yourself in today. What makes it difficult for you?
- What would you need to do in order to rest in your desert?
- Underline James 1:2–4, Hebrews 12:7–11, and Romans 8:38–39 in your copy of God's Word.

Discussion Questions

1. Share a desert experience you've already survived. Share what God taught you through it.

2. Take turns describing what a rest in your desert might look like.

3. Have you been able to praise God in spite of your desert? How did you get to that place? What resulted from being able to do that?

4. What will the end of your desert experience possibly look like?

Treasure Verse

Forget the former things; do not dwell on the past. See, I am doing a new thing! Now it springs up; do you not perceive it? I am making a way in the wilderness and streams in the wasteland.

Isaiah 43:18–19

14

Great Expectations

Woe to those who quarrel with their Maker, those who are nothing but potsherds among the potsherds on the ground. Does the clay say to the potter, "What are you making?" Does your work say, "The potter has no hands"?

Isaiah 45:9

A few years ago I was asked to lead sessions at a conference teaching the characteristics of the baby boomer generation and giving ideas for ministry to boomers. I titled one of my classes "Great Expectations." In that class I explained that one characteristic of the boomer generation was the expectation that life would be good, and that if we wanted it to stay that way all we had to do was posture ourselves for blessing. The only problem with that train of thought is that it eventually runs out of track. I know that you know this to be true, otherwise you wouldn't be reading a book with the subtitle "Finding direction and peace through the struggles of life."

Therefore, I want to share with you some of the truths I shared in that class. I began each session with a case study. For this one I shared my own story.

Meet Me

I am at the very end of the boomer generation (and because of that I have many Gen X characteristics). I was born in 1963, and although I was only an infant when John F. Kennedy was shot, I know exactly where I was (I've heard the story told over and over). My school years began in 1969 and culminated in 1981—with the bulk of my public school education being in the decade of the '70s. Civil rights continued to advance, the anti-war movement escalated, Richard Nixon resigned from the presidency, the women's movement was on the rise, and abortion was made legal. With so much "freedom of choice and speech," we truly believed that we could determine our destiny, weave our own dreams—and if we wanted to know our mood, we wore a ring.

I was saved when I was eleven years old, and I learned to have a daily quiet time, to witness to friends, and to lead in the church as a teen growing up in a youth group that took discipleship seriously. So my life philosophy was a mixture of culture and church. I embraced Jeremiah 29:11 as my life verse and trusted God to prosper me as I continued on the adventure He had for my life. And prosper me He did, until I was faced with infertility as a young pastor's wife. Not being able to become pregnant with a child was the first time I'd not gotten what I wanted, and oh, how I pitched a fit about it! But in time God granted my heart's desire, and I became the mother of three. Life once again was filled with abundance and goodness and all that I could possibly imagine (even more) until 2010.

In 2010, I started teaching weekly lessons on spiritual warfare as I began writing *Spiritual Warfare for Women*. As I've mentioned before, soon afterward my life seemed to unravel. The following year was kinder and gentler, but you already know that my cancer returned in May of 2012. I had great expectations of life until these very real struggles shook me to my core.

What Our Parents Failed to Tell Us

I discovered that I wasn't the only one with "great expectations." Most people I know live with the same. I read an excellent article that explained one writer's opinion of why we boomers tend to embrace such lofty ideals. (Though I don't think this way of thinking is unique to boomers.) Let me share a few of his insights with you here.

The writer, Mike Bella, says, "In my 1988 book, *Baby Boom Believers,* I point out that one of the causes for our high childhood expectations was something our parents told us, or more accurately, failed to tell us." Bella goes on to say that our parents told us how lucky we were because they considered our culture much kinder compared to the one they experienced (littered with the Great Depression and the Great War). They wanted to instill in us an attitude of gratitude, but instead we developed a sense of entitlement.

Bella says that our parents should have done a better job of preparing us for the realities of pain and suffering that are part of the human experience. "Parents should have concluded their talks with us with admonitions to develop both gratefulness and toughness. The first we would need to enjoy life; the second, to survive it."[1]

But even if they had warned us to expect difficult times, we probably would not have listened. How many times did my mother—and every other woman whose children were grown—look me in the eyes, when my three were preschoolers, and tell me not to wish away the moments? I remember them urging me to cherish each and every minute of potty training, finger painting, and puppy dog parties! Did I heed their words? No! In my mind those three couldn't get to college fast enough. That was until they reached

1. Mike Bella, *Best Years,* "What Our Parents Never Told Us," accessed March 1, 2013, www.bestyears.com/parentstold.html.

their senior year in high school. *Then* I cried out for a screeching halt and begged to turn back the hands of time. We tend to ignore the wisdom of our elders until we *are* the elders.

The Natural Result of Living With Unmet Expectations

As a result of these great expectations, when life happens we spin our wheels and thus dig a deeper rut. Here are the ways that we stay stuck in the mud of disappointment and confusion.

We become victims.

I tell my children often that a victim mentality is a yielding of power. When we think and feel like victims (thoughts lead to feelings), we give up any power to do anything about the way we will respond to our circumstances. Rather than agree with God's Word in Romans 8:28, we sit back and sing, "Gloom, despair, and agony on me, woooaaaah!"

We despair.

And how does this reflect the glory of God? The minute we make the joy and success of our lives dependent on our circumstances is the minute we begin to worship a lesser god. If we give our peace of mind over to the ins and outs of life on earth, we chain ourselves to the prince of this world. Colossians 2:6–8 warns us against doing this.

> So then, just as you have received Christ Jesus as Lord, continue to live in him, rooted and built up in him, strengthened in the faith as you were taught, and overflowing with thankfulness. See to it that no one takes you captive through hollow and deceptive philosophy, which depends on human tradition and the basic principles of this world rather than on Christ.

As children of God, we are urged to live our lives "in Christ," not "in the world."

We become narcissistic.

Narcissism is excessive self-love. Being consumed with your own feelings, needs, hurts, unfulfilled desires, or disappointments blinds you to the feelings, needs, hurts, desires, and disappointments of others. Jesus urged us to deny ourselves, not to spend our lives searching for ways to fulfill ourselves! A life that is consumed with self is a life that is missing its purpose.

We isolate ourselves from others.

Oftentimes, as a defense mechanism, the response to hurt is to isolate oneself from people who might hurt us. In the movie *Ghosts of Girlfriends Past* (a modern retelling of the Charles Dickens' classic *A Christmas Carol*), the main character, Connor Mead, a rather narcissistic bachelor, has a radical change of heart and mind after spending a sleepless night with various ghosts. In a desperate attempt to save his brother's marriage, Connor chases after his future sister-in-law's car as she and her bridesmaids are headed to the airport after calling off the wedding. Upon gaining her attention, he warns her of the loneliness that results from running away from hurt (or the potential of hurt) in loving relationships with others. These are his words:

> It doesn't mean that you're never going to get hurt, but the pain you feel will never compare to the regret that comes from walking away from love. And from someone who's felt a lot of both—trust me, regret beats pain every day of the week and twice on Sunday. Don't run away. Don't do it.
>
> Connor Mead in *Ghosts of Girlfriends Past*

We regress.

Perhaps you've heard it said that our Christian walk is three steps forward and two steps back. Wouldn't it be great if we could so bow under the mighty hand of God that when our expectations are crushed we simply stand firm and trust God to use that disappointment to hurl us forward?

My father enjoys working in the yard at our house in the North Carolina Mountains. We have rhododendron growing in front of the house, but they never looked very healthy. Instead of having thick leaves they were tall and spindly. A few summers ago Tom and I went up to our house and were surprised to see those rhododendron bushes severely pruned. I knew that my dad had gotten after them. My mother told me that she fussed and fussed at him for killing them. But the next year, in the spring, those bushes were thicker and healthier than they'd ever been. In keeping with Jesus' teaching in John 15, the pruning, which seemed harmful and severe at the time, produced growth—healthy, strong growth.

When our expectations are crushed, perhaps the Master Gardener is pruning us. What might happen if we yielded to His shears and trusted that in due season we will produce much fruit?

We lose faith.

When some people encounter a hard disappointment, they give up on expecting God to do anything wonderful ever again. They become sour and negative. They let the disappointments in this life blind them to the treasures God hides in dark places. Like Peter, they get all confused. Don't let this happen to you. When the struggles of life come your way, put on the full armor of God and stand firm (see Ephesians 6:10–18)!

We live in a constant state of discontent.

You know these people. They come to church on Sunday and mumble the words along with you when you sing the praise songs, but then they leave with their heads hung down and their eyes focused on the floor. If you ask them how they're doing, they speak in a lonely voice about how they're barely making it. They remind me of Eeyore, the sad little donkey in the stories of Winnie the Pooh.

> "Good morning, Pooh Bear," said Eeyore gloomily. "If it *is* a good morning," he said. "Which I doubt," said he.
> "Why, what's the matter?"
> "Nothing, Pooh Bear, nothing. We can't all, and some of us don't. That's all there is to it."
> "Can't all *what*?" said Pooh, rubbing his nose.
> "Gaiety. Song-and-dance. Here we go round the mulberry bush."[2]

He's kind of cute in the stories, but shouldn't a child of God be more like Tigger than Eeyore?

Trouble in Getting to Solla Sollew

I hope that even if you're not a baby boomer you understand the difference between living with great expectations and accepting the limits of life in a fallen world. I hope that by now you understand that, as a child of the King of Kings, nothing comes into your life (or goes out of it) that does not first get filtered through His supreme wisdom and perfect love. I also hope that you understand that God hides precious treasures in the dark places (smack-dab in the middle of struggles that threaten to crush you), and only when you choose to go spelunking with Him will you find them.

As you can already tell, I've learned how to listen to the voice of God even through the means of entertainment: movies, children's

2. A. A. Milne, *Winnie the Pooh* (New York: Penguin, 2006), 77.

books, lyrics in songs, etc. And there is much in Dr. Seuss that reflects truth. In his book *I Had Trouble in Getting to Solla Sollew,* he tells the story of a fella who sought to run away from the troubles in his life. He'd heard of a city called Solla Sollew, where "they never have troubles, at least very few." So he set off to find it, and after dealing with more trouble than you or I would care to press through, he finally made it to the doors of the city. With celebration he proclaimed,

> I'd made it! I'd done it! At last I was there! And I knew that I'd left all my troubles behind when a chap at a doorway . . . waved me a wave that was friendly and kind.
>
> "Welcome!" he said as he gave me his hand. . . . "Welcome to sweet, sunny Solla Sollew, where we never have troubles. At least very few. As a matter of fact, we have only just one. . . .
>
> "Imagine! Just one little trouble, my son. And this one little trouble, as you will now see, is this one little trouble I have with this key. . . ."[3]

After all of his trouble, the poor fellow was stuck outside the city with no way in because of a Key-Slapping Slippard who kept the door locked. I couldn't help but think that we are so much like him. We have these great expectations that life should be without troubles (at least very few), and we spend countless days sidestepping disappointment, overcoming obstacles, and pressing on to find a place where we can sit back and celebrate a life that is free of suffering, anguish, and pain. Only that place does not exist, not here and not now. The purpose of life is to follow God's plans, not to avoid pain.

Jeremiah 29:11 says, "'For I know the plans I have for you,' declares the Lord."

Do you want God to supernaturally bless your own plans—or are you willing to submit all that you have to invest in His plan? The poor

3. Dr. Seuss, *I Had Trouble in Getting to Solla Sollew* (New York: Random House, 1965).

old chap who was plagued by troubles spent many long days and nights traveling to Solla Sollew because he was promised an escape from his troubles. And when he arrived, a small Key-Slapping Slippard destroyed his plan. Woman of God, let me assure you that while your life might have more than its fair share of ups and downs, God has a plan. He has a plan for you. But here's the thing: It's His plan.

What Does God's Plan Look Like?

One morning when I was walking, I sensed God say this to my spirit, *"Leighann! When Isaiah spoke the words in chapter 40:1–2, he was prophesying the coming of Christ.* [I knew that already.] *But realize that when he declared that prophecy, neither Isaiah nor anyone who heard him speak those words lived long enough to see them come true."*

Hmm. Imagine that, spending your entire life telling people what you heard from God, and neither you nor they live long enough to know if you told the truth! That was a powerful reminder to me that God's plans are not limited to 60, 70, or even 120 years. His plans are not limited to my life-span. God went on to tell me this: *"In fact, most everyone in the Bible who followed hard after me didn't have a clue how their obedience would impact my kingdom work. And their obedience oftentimes cost them dearly. But each one of them was willing to sacrifice their own plans, their own glory, and their own earthly experience to invest in my kingdom plan."*

I answered God back, "So the plans you have for me, the ones you promised me in Jeremiah 29:11, they're *your* plans, not mine; for *your* glory, not mine. Hmm." I had to think about that for a while.

After that conversation with God I began to come to grips with a different expectation. Rather than have great expectations that centered around my happiness, comfort, and joy, I began to understand that my life's purpose was to participate in God's ongoing plan. I saw His plan like a mighty river with a strong and steady current. I used to think that my life was a little creek off to the side of that river and that God's plans flowed into my little creek, tickling my pebbles and cooling my toes. But as I thought about God, about how He was in the beginning and will be in the end, I realized that my life was not a little creek. In some marvelous way, the life I live here on earth will impact the kingdom to come. But it's not the little ripples that are going to make a difference, it's the powerful flow of the constant steady current of God's plan. If I want my life to matter, if I don't want my pain to be wasted, then I'll get out of the creek and dive into the river and trust God to keep my head above water as I move through life with Him.

Have *great expectations* for your life! You would dishonor God if you didn't. But let those expectations bow low under the mighty hand of God. Embrace ministry to others that comes right out of the disillusionment that is birthed when life crushes your dreams. Show them God and help them to understand the incredible joy of letting God use the struggles of their own lives to demonstrate His power and His love.

Treasure Hunt

Personal Reflection

- Which one of the seven natural results of unmet great expectations do you gravitate toward?
- What is the difference between expecting God to bless your plans and throwing yourself headlong into His plans?

Discussion Questions

1. Share unmet great expectations that have happened in your life. Tell how those experiences affected you and your journey with God.

2. What might your life look like if you were completely immersed in God's plans rather than your own?

3. How have you allowed the disappointments in your life to lead you to ministry?

Treasure Verse

I know that everything God does will endure forever; nothing can be added to it and nothing taken from it. God does it so that people will fear him.

Ecclesiastes 3:14

15

My Story . . . God's Glory

They overcame him by the blood of the Lamb and by the word of
their testimony.

Revelation 12:11 NKJV

According to Proverbs 13:12, "Hope deferred makes the heart
sick." But even when hope is deferred, God is at work. God
has worked and is working in your life, purposefully preparing a
way for you to best share Him with others. You may have heard it
said that without a test there would be no testimony. Throughout
this book I've shared such tests. Now it's time for you to consider
your own. Some serious pondering and beholding will enable you
to coauthor, with your Creator, the rest of your story. Learn how
to be God's mirror reflecting His glory through your life, one line
at a time.

Ministering Through Your Life Story

I hope that by now you've learned how to recognize the voice of
God in the middle of life's most difficult circumstances. Woven in
and out of every chapter of this book is a subtle challenge for you

to discover the adventure that God has for those who love and trust Him. I hope you are discovering that adventure.

I have another friend who lost her newborn infant. Her baby was born with a rare chromosome disorder. She and her husband had no forewarning; they were faced with their daughter's grim future at her birth. She lived only a few days. As I shared before, the death of babies is one of the hardest things we've had to face as pastors. But several years have passed, and my friend is a great woman of faith who allowed God to weave His comfort through her heart. So when we decided to begin a ministry to women who'd lost children, she volunteered to lead the group. I told her how proud I was of her willingness to serve. She responded to my praise with this simple, straightforward comment: "Well, I figure if I'm going to have to experience it, I want God to get glory out of it." When she said it, my heart broke for her. But in seeing her strength and conviction, I could not deny that God was somehow healing her wound as He invited her to participate in His eternal purpose.

Her attitude has been my banner. If I'm going to have to go through it, then I'm going to make sure God gets glory from it! No matter what *it* is. In this chapter I am going to show you how to write your own story for God's glory. Then I'm going to leave you with some practical suggestions for how you might share your story with others.

Step 1: Connect the Dots Backward

Honestly, this is where age is an advantage. It's only after you've experienced many years of being an adult that you can look back and connect the dots to see how God was meticulously and methodically working His plan in and through your life all along the way. But don't be discouraged if you're not "old" yet. As you consider the struggles you've endured, ask God to give you a heavenly perspective on them.

My son, TJ, brought home an article about Steve Jobs, the former CEO of Apple Computer and Pixar Entertainment. The article was actually a commencement address he delivered at Stanford University in 2005. As he spoke to the graduates, he shared several pivotal moments in his life. These included dropping out of college after six months and dropping into a calligraphy class that eventually led to a major impact on the design of Macintosh computers. Jobs shared,

> None of this had even a hope of any practical application in my life. But ten years later, when we were designing the first Macintosh computer, it all came back to me. And we designed it all into the Mac. It was the first computer with beautiful typography. If I had never dropped in on that single course in college, the Mac would have never had multiple typefaces or proportionally spaced fonts. And since Windows just copied the Mac, it's likely that no personal computer would have them. If I had never dropped out, I would have never dropped in on this calligraphy class, and personal computers might not have the wonderful typography that they do.[1]

He continued by sharing that he was fired by the board of directors from the company he started in his parents' garage (Apple), but how that firing ended up being one of the best things that ever happened to him. He went on to create another company, Pixar (the creators of animated movies such as *Toy Story*), and he met his wife. As he continued, he told the students that they needed to learn the art of connecting the dots of their lives backward.

The first step to telling your life story is to connect the dots backward. Consider the people and circumstances that have impacted your life to bring you to the place that you are today. Steve Jobs narrowed it down to just a few. This is important to do—just consider those people and events that intersected your path and perhaps changed your course.

1. *Stanford News,* " 'You've got to find what you love,' Jobs says," June 14, 2005, http://news.stanford.edu/news/2005/june15/jobs-061505.html.

The story of Joseph is a great biblical example of connecting the dots backward. His story is found in Genesis 37, 39–51. We discussed it already in chapter 7. If Joseph were connecting his dots backward, the dots would be the telling of his dreams; his brothers' tossing him in a pit but then selling him into slavery; life as a slave in Potiphar's house, and being wrongly accused; life in the dungeon; the interpretation of the dreams of the baker and cupbearer; the interpretation of Pharaoh's dream; the famine; the encounter with his brothers and father; saving his family from starvation; and then full reconciliation with his brothers.

I encourage you to connect the dots backward by listing them on a sheet of paper. Beside each one write a sentence or two explaining why you chose that "dot."

Step 2: Identify God's Glory Along the Way

This is such a great practice to get into! All along your journey through life you can trace the hand and the heart of God. But sometimes you are so overwhelmed by the challenge of your circumstances that if you are not diligent, the Enemy will convince you that God has less than your best interest in mind. And when you let Satan do that to you, when you entertain doubt and begin to disregard the truth of God's faithfulness and love, you will become blind to all that He is doing in the midst of your mess.

But when you choose to take those devilish thoughts captive to the lordship of Christ like you are encouraged to do in 2 Corinthians 10:5, then you will begin to see the intricate working of the glory of God in your own life. Once you begin to see God's glory shining through the shards of your broken dreams, you will be like the woman at the well; you will not be able to help but shout His glory to others! You will be eager to share your story. "Come and meet the man who has been intimately involved in even the details of my life!" (see John 4:29) you will shout as you go.

Think about one of the most painful experiences you've had. What did you learn through that experience? How did God reveal himself to you in it? What did He teach you about His love? In time, did He prove himself faithful to a promise? Which promise and how? These are the questions you want to answer as you record your story.

I'll give you one for me. I shared with you that I was infertile. During my journey through infertility, I learned what it meant to surrender my dreams and my plans to the dreams and plans God had for me. Eventually I became pregnant, but it took several years. During those years I worked full time in a job where I was invited to write articles and curriculum. I attended writers' conferences for free and developed my writing skills. I've dreamed of being a writer since I was twelve years old. And that job opened the professional writing world to me. Not only that, but during those years our little congregation grew from eight to about 120 people. Because we were in such a small church, my paycheck provided for Tom and me our insurance and groceries. Through the years that I struggled with infertility, I learned that prayer was relationship, not the delivery of a wish list. Several years after God answered my cry for children, I wrote the prayer study that birthed the ministry I'm still engaged in today. Even now I am writing books that were birthed through those years with my *Oh God, Please!* series of prayer books. Then, after God blessed Tom and me with two baby girls and a boy, I knew by experience that He is capable of doing exceedingly, abundantly more than I could ever ask or imagine! On this side of infertility I see God's faithfulness and His wisdom. *That* is a story I enjoy telling.

But what if you are not on the other side of your answered prayer? When you can walk in such complete trust and faith in the wisdom and love of God that you don't have to be on the other side of the work He is completing in you; when you can declare His glory before He is done . . . oh, my dear sister, you are all the more able to let Him reveal himself through you every step of the way.

Second Corinthians 1:20 says this:

For no matter how many promises God has made, they are "Yes" in Christ. And so through Him the "Amen" is spoken by us to the glory of God.

When we believe that we have received the fulfillment of God's promises before they are actualized, and before they are recognized by nonbelievers—*that* is when we say *"So be it"* to the glory of God! When we live our lives as if God has already answered our heart cries—with joy, confidence, assurance, and peace—then we are living in contrast to the world. Then we are demonstrating our confidence in the God we know is able.

Consider journaling what you are going through, asking God to show you His glory along the way. Keep a record of what He teaches you about himself. Be careful to recognize how He responds to your prayers. Record the many ways He reveals himself to you.

Step 3: Explain God's Character as He Has Revealed It to You

Finally, when you tell your story, explain what one thing God has shown you about himself. There is nothing more encouraging to a woman struggling in her faith than for a woman like you to wrap your arm around her and tell her that you *know* that God is able because . . . (and you tell her your story).

What has God revealed to you about himself? What characteristic or promise has He undeniably communicated to you? What characteristic or promise is He communicating to you right now? These are the questions to ask yourself as you record God's glory as He's revealed himself to you in your life's story.

Until I was diagnosed with cancer I never knew (not really) how I would face my own mortality. I wanted to believe that I would go to heaven when I died, I just really didn't want to die to get there. Death wasn't something I pondered very often. Heaven was some other place that I'd think more about when I got old. During the first fifteen minutes after Dr. Caudill spoke the terrible words "You have cancer," when I didn't know if I would live or die, I went from the shock of the unimaginable happening to me to a calm, supernatural realization that I know, I know, I know that my eternity is safe in the nail-scarred hands of Jesus. In those minutes God revealed to me that He is life, and that eternal life is a free gift that I have definitely received through Jesus His Son.

What has God revealed to you about himself? Be ready to share this as often as God gives you opportunity.

Some Advice From a Writer

With these simple steps you can write your story. But unless you set time aside and do the hard work of facing a blank piece of paper with pen in hand, you will not get it written. At some point you just have to get started. The best way I know to get my story written is to set aside time when I can get away from the distractions of my everyday life and focus on the one task of writing. I'm doing that right now.

You may not have the luxury of actually going away, but you can still get away from distractions at home by turning off your phone and shutting down the Internet. I am not very good at writing when I'm distracted by the jingle I hear on my computer when someone sends me an email or Facebook message. So I turn those things off when I write. If you write for an hour or two a day, you will have your story recorded in no time. Of course my favorite way to write is to be able to set aside an entire day (or week), but you are writing a story, not a book.

Where and how to share your stories once they are written.

I hope you will continue to take time to write your stories. Here are some practical ideas for ways that you can write and share your own stories and encourage others to write and share theirs with you.

1. Host a writing retreat. Invite women who enjoy writing and who need to get away to reflect on the ways that God has spoken to them in their current circumstances. Spend time at your retreat worshiping God. Share your stories with one another, and when you share those stories, encourage one another! Then spend blocks of time alone writing your stories. Make it a goal to have a time of praise at the end of the retreat for the way God has been (and is being) faithful to you right now.

2. Plan an event where you invite women to share their stories as related to specific things: broken marriages, aging parents, challenging children, etc. Do this in a coffee-shop-type setting. But before you give one another free rein with a microphone, practice together. Make sure that each person shares her story from a positive, God-glorifying perspective. Also, give each storyteller a time limit, and make sure that she honors it. I do this by asking each woman to write her story out word-for-word and email it to me before the event. I can tell how long she will speak based on her notes. See appendix 3 for a guide to help you plan your event.

3. Invite women to share testimonies in your Bible study groups or weekly women's gatherings. The men in our church practice this at their weekly get-together on Wednesday nights. For twenty to thirty minutes they take turns sharing how God is answering prayers in their lives. The men tell their stories, and through those stories other men are challenged to overcome difficulties in their own lives. Consider capturing testimonies on video and sharing them in small groups.

4. Share your story one-on-one. This is most likely the best and most powerful way God will use it. Share it often and learn to listen as the person you are sharing with opens up to share hers with you.

A Word About Listening

This story-telling ministry is just as powerful whether you are the sharer or the listener. Women who are struggling with their own "stuff" will be encouraged to hear your story, but they will also be encouraged when you sit still and quiet to listen to others share theirs. I cannot tell you how much it has meant to me to have friends who will listen. Therefore I want to leave you with five tips for developing your listening skills.

In order to be a good listener:

1. **Pay attention.** Have you ever talked with someone who doesn't seem to be paying attention to what you are saying? If so, you know what to do in order to pay attention. Maintain eye contact and nod your head or express your understanding with appropriate responses. Ask questions like, "What did you do next?" and "What did she say then?" Be careful to be genuinely engaged in what the person is saying, and not preoccupied with composing clever replies. Also be careful not to interrupt or distract the speaker in the middle of her thoughts.

2. **Shut out distractions.** Let the person talking know that what she has to say is more important than the book you are reading or the television program you are watching. But also shut out the distracting thoughts that bombard your mind. The best way to do this is to engage your heart. Try to imagine what your friend is feeling as she shares her story.

3. **Be careful not to pass judgment.** It is easy to begin evaluating and even judging the speaker if you're not careful. Try to keep an open mind.

   This is especially important when people are hurting. I've been reading Job in my quiet time and have almost laughed out loud at the ignorance of his friends. Several times they felt like they had to straighten Job out when all he really wanted and needed was a safe place to vent. One great verse to keep in mind is Job 13:5: "If only you would be altogether silent! For you, that would be wisdom." I think that this is what many of us want to say to well-meaning friends who are overly eager to tell us how we ought or ought not to be feeling. Be careful not to do that.

4. **Resist the urge to share your own story.** Sometimes our friends get to the part of the story that parallels our own and we suddenly stop listening to them and instead try to tell them our story. As a listener, your ministry is being there so they can put their thoughts and feelings into words. Even if you can empathize with them, let them own the story. When they are done you might share tiny snippets of the ways that your experiences give you compassion for them.

5. **Respond carefully and candidly.** Feel free to make statements for clarification such as, "I hear you saying . . ." This is a great way to diffuse tension if you and the speaker are trying to find a solution to conflict. By repeating it back in your own words, the speaker will know that you were listening. The quickest way to diffuse a conflict between yourself and another is to seek to understand and be understood. The only way you can do this is to listen and learn.

Be candid and honest in your response, always maintaining respect for the speaker. Recognize that what the speaker is feeling is more powerful than what she is saying. So respond to her feelings when possible.

Listening to the Voice of God

This book is all about learning to hear the voice of God. What an appropriate way to conclude . . . with five tips for effective listening. What if we took those tips and applied them to our relationship with God? Let's see what happens.

1. Pay attention. What might happen if you met the Lord first thing in the morning, every morning? What if you opened your

Bible, asked God to speak to you through it, and listened to what He had to say? What might happen if you allowed enough time in this place to sit very still and not say a thing? Try it! Being still and quiet when I met the Lord in His Word radically improved my prayer life.

Of course we don't get to have a physical audience with God. But can't we catch a glimpse of His glory by soaking in creation? Take time to look at the sky, the nature that surrounds you, anything that reflects the handiwork of God. You can't see Him, but you can see where He's been and what He's created. Learn to see people as God's unique masterpieces. Marvel in their individuality and celebrate the work of God's hands.

2. Shut out distractions. Turn off the TV! Put down your phone. Stop tweeting, Facebooking, and texting. Focus on the lost art of being present in the moment, even if the moment is quiet. Settle your inner thoughts by keeping a piece of paper handy while you're having your quiet time. When outside thoughts come to mind, jot them down. This way you will not be distracted by trying to remember things while you are praying, reading the Bible, and being still enough to hear God's voice.

3. Be careful not to pass judgment. While we may not see ourselves passing judgment on God, we might be guilty of coming into His presence with preconceived notions. For instance, the other day I was talking with a woman who is extremely unhappy in her marriage, and she said to me, "God wants me to be happy, doesn't He?" Does He? I reminded her that while God cares about us deeply, He is much more interested in our holiness than He is in our happiness.

God is always teaching you new things and expanding your understanding of Him and His ways. Allow Him to rearrange your preconceived notions and correct your wrong thinking. I can't tell you how many times God has done this in me over the past two years.

4. Resist the urge to share your own story. Be careful when praying not to do all the talking. Sometimes I think God would like to say, "I need you to be quiet! You're talking so much I can't get a word in edgewise!"

5. Respond carefully and candidly. When you spend time with God, you learn to recognize His voice. I've shared a few excerpts from my prayer life where I've told you what I heard God saying to me. I've grown to "hear" His voice through years of following the principles and instructions He's given us in His Word. Even then I make sure that what I am hearing lines up with what is written in the Bible. I don't want to be tricked into thinking I'm hearing the voice of God when I'm just imagining things.

James tells us the difference between merely "listening to" God's Word and actually *hearing* it. Those who hear . . . do.

> But don't just listen to God's word. You must *do what it says.* Otherwise, you are only fooling yourselves. For if you listen to the word and don't obey, it is like glancing at your face in a mirror. You see yourself, walk away, and forget what you look like. But if you look carefully into the perfect law that sets you free, and *if you do what it says* and don't forget what you heard, then God will bless you for doing it.
>
> James 1:22–25 NLT

You will learn to hear God's voice when you learn to obey His Word. And as you walk in obedience to His Word, you will grow in your confidence of hearing His still, small voice.

Wrapping Up My Story

A few years ago Karen messaged me on Facebook. She and I were friends in high school, but after graduation our paths parted and we went our separate ways. It had been nearly thirty years since I'd heard from her. Her story alone was enough to encourage me, but the timing of it was a direct message from God to me. I received her message on March 8. That morning I'd had a colonoscopy (one that had to be done one year after my cancer diagnosis just to make sure no cancer was left behind). I'd looked forward to the colonoscopy for one reason only—the drug they give you creates this sense of euphoric sleep. I'd never experienced anything like it until my colonoscopies the year before. Each time I was given that "happy sleeping" drug, I woke up feeling like I hadn't a care in the world. This was the effect this drug had on me (and on many other people, I'm told). On this particular day I longed for that feeling—for the things going on in my world were breaking my heart, and I longed for an escape from it even if my escape was temporary and drug-induced.

However, the drug didn't work that way on that day. I guess the heaviness in my spirit was too much for that little drug. I awoke crying rather than laughing. By the time the effects of being put to sleep were wearing off (in the afternoon), I kind of wondered why God didn't allow me that one little reprieve from the heartache I'd been suffering for a year. I opened my computer, logged on to Facebook, and found this message:

THANK YOU!!!

Hey Leighann,

I write this and should have written earlier. There is not much I can say on that, but I just didn't.

Over the years, God has put you on my mind to pray for, and in the past few months even more so. I write to share two things that may encourage you:

1. You probably don't know this, but when I was 15 I was going to commit suicide. But that day I saw a friend at school (that would be you). Going to church and knowing God seemed to make her different . . . that is part of my testimony. I asked my parents to take me to church. They did not go, and I think they were shocked that I was even speaking to them. My dad mainly yelled at me, and my mom did little to defend me. But they took me to church and I got saved one morning—April 8, when I was 15. After attending for a few months, I heard one particular Scripture—Revelation

3:20. I was shocked God loved me, I was shocked God loved me and died for me. . . . That is the beginning of my testimony.

My parents are now strong and dedicated Christians, thanks to this turn of events, and we are best of friends now. I've wanted over the years to tell you THANK YOU. When I mentioned it to a friend, they said, "Why don't you see if she is on Facebook?" That is why I looked for you a few weeks ago.

2. I also write to say that a week or so ago, God gave me a dream about you and just asked me to pray for you. The short of it is to pray God would encourage you. I sensed He wanted you to know that He knows what's going on with you and hasn't forgotten.

Well, I could write more, but I mainly wanted to say THANK YOU. Without your witness in high school, I probably wouldn't be here. I wouldn't be a Christian, my parents wouldn't be Christians, my niece and nephew wouldn't be [Christians] (still waiting on one nephew), and countless other things (other real miracles) would not have happened as well. One life does affect more than you know. I hope you know a little more just how much now.

I leave with one of my favorite quotes from Henrietta Mears. She is the lady who started graded curriculum in Sunday school, built a retreat center, shepherded Bill Bright and his wife, and was the most influential person to Billy Graham other than his mother and wife. In short, God used her greatly. When asked at the end of her life what she would have done differently, she responded, "I would have trusted Christ more." I pray God continues to do more in and through your life than even you may know.

THANK YOU AGAIN!!! Karen

God used me in Karen's life many years ago and I didn't even know it. I had no idea that her home life was rough or that she contemplated suicide. I didn't even know when she was saved! And I certainly didn't know that I had that kind of impact on her coming to know the Lord. But for reasons known only to God, He determined to encourage me by waiting until March 8—over thirty years after her conversion experience—to give me that encouragement. What was so cool about Karen's message was that God used her to speak His word to me. God knew that I needed to know that He hadn't forgotten me and that He was fully aware of what was going on with me. He also knew that if I would just "trust Christ more," I wouldn't suffer so.

While I was writing this chapter of my book, Karen messaged me again. This time she told me about seeing a picture of a wall we'd painted at our church—the one where we printed the many names of God. Right in the center of that wall is printed **I AM.** Karen shared with me that the Lord used that picture to remind her that if we would just focus on *who God is,* we wouldn't have such a difficult time trusting Him, believing Him, obeying Him, and experiencing Him. She was preparing for a retreat and told me how she was going to share our story with the women there.

I asked her if I could share our story here and if I could have the honor of closing my book with that great admonition. Hearing God's voice is not rocket science. It's not even new math. All you have to do is "trust Christ more" and embrace the great **I AM!**

Treasure Hunt

Personal Reflection

- Consider planning a place and a time to write your story.
  I will write my story _____ (when)
  at _____ (where).

Discussion Questions

1. Which of the listening skills do you most need to develop?
2. How might developing these skills help you to better hear the voice of God?
3. Have you ever had an experience like mine, when God uses a person or a situation to speak a specific word to you? Share that experience with your group.

Treasure Verse

They overcame him by the blood of the Lamb and by the word of their testimony.

Revelation 12:11 NKJV

Appendix 1

Promises to Claim

These are the promises I printed on Post-it Notes and placed throughout my house when I found myself at the ford of the Jabbok during the summer of 2010. Most of them have to do with promises related to our children and our children's children, because those were the issues I was dealing with. They are in no particular order.

> I remain confident of this; I will see the goodness of the Lord in the land of the living. Wait for the Lord; be strong and take heart and wait for the Lord.
>
> Psalm 27:13–14

> "Though the mountains be shaken and the hills be removed, yet my unfailing love for you will not be shaken nor my covenant of peace be removed," says the Lord who has compassion on you.
>
> Isaiah 54:10

> Forget the former things; do not dwell on the past. See, I am doing a new thing! Now it springs up; do you not perceive it? I am making a way in the wilderness and streams in the wasteland.
>
> Isaiah 43:18–19

"As for me, this is my covenant with them," says the Lord. "My Spirit, who is on you, will not depart from you, and my words that I have put in your mouth will always be on your lips, on the lips of your children and on the lips of their descendants—from this time on and forever."

Isaiah 59:21

But now, this is what the Lord says—he who created you, Jacob, he who formed you, Israel: "Do not fear, for I have redeemed you; I have summoned you by name; you are mine."

Isaiah 43:1

I was young and now I am old, yet I have never seen the righteous forsaken or their children begging bread.

Psalm 37:25

"Is not my word like fire," declares the Lord, "and like a hammer that breaks a rock in pieces?"

Jeremiah 23:29

This is the confidence we have in approaching God: that if we ask anything according to his will, he hears us. And if we know that he hears us—whatever we ask—we know that we have what we asked of him.

1 John 5:14–15

I will say to the north, "Give them up!" and to the south, "Do not hold them back." Bring my sons from afar and my daughters from the ends of the earth.

Isaiah 43:6

All your children will be taught by the Lord, and great will be their peace.

Isaiah 54:13

In my distress I prayed to the Lord, and the Lord answered me and set me free.

Psalm 118:5 NLT

I was pushed back and about to fall, but the Lord helped me. The Lord is my strength and my defense; he has become my salvation.

Psalm 118:13–14 (This is the verse Tom preached from at Melissa and David's son's memorial service.)

I will make an everlasting covenant with them: I will never stop doing good to them, and I will inspire them to fear me, so that they will never turn away from me.

Jeremiah 32:40

"The glory of this present house will be greater than the glory of the former house," says the Lord Almighty. "And in this place I will grant peace," declares the Lord Almighty.

Haggai 2:9 (This is the verse my daughter Kaleigh showed me.)

Do not be afraid, for I am with you; I will bring your children from the east and gather you from the west.

Isaiah 43:5

I will rejoice in doing them good and will assuredly plant them in this land with all my heart and soul.

Jeremiah 32:41

I know that you are pleased with me, for my enemy does not triumph over me.

Psalm 41:11

Why, my soul, are you downcast? Why so disturbed within me? Put your hope in God, for I will yet praise him, my Savior and my God.

Psalm 43:5

Shouts of joy and victory resound in the tents of the righteous; the Lord's right hand has done mighty things!

Psalm 118:15

Surely the arm of the Lord is not too short to save, nor his ear too dull to hear.

Isaiah 59:1

My eyes will watch over them for their good, and I will bring them back to this land. I will build them up and not tear them down; I will plant them and not uproot them. I will give them a heart to know me, that I am the Lord. They will be my people, and I will be their God, for they will return to me with all their heart.

Jeremiah 24:6–7

Appendix 2

Outline My Story/God's Glory

Use this outline to write your story for God's glory.

Step 1: Connect the Dots Backward

Try to think of at least five times in your life when something happened to move you in a certain direction. Jot down two or three sentences to explain why you chose that particular event.

•

•

•

•

•

Step 2: Identify God's Glory Along the Way

As you consider the five events above, answer these questions for each one.

1. What did you learn through that experience?
2. How did God reveal himself to you in it?
3. What did He teach you about His love?
4. In time, did He prove himself faithful to a promise? Which promise and how?

Step 3: Explain God's Character as He Has Revealed It to You

Take one of the five events you have identified and answer the following questions. These will help you identify what part of God's character He revealed to you through that experience. After you do this with one event, do it with the others.

1. What has God revealed to you about himself?
2. What characteristic or promise has He undeniably communicated to you?
3. What characteristic or promise is He communicating to you right now?

Where to Share Your Story

(Event-Planning Guide
for Women's Ministry Leaders)

I gave you a list of ways that you might offer women opportunities to share their stories. Here is an event-planning guide for a coffee-shop-type event designed to share stories.

Six Months Before Your Event

- Determine your date and secure your location (book it on the church calendar).
- Choose a theme.
- Determine your budget (and decide how you will pay—from the church budget? From ticket sales? From donations?).
- Review technical needs and enlist technicians (PowerPoint, sound, etc.).
- Determine how you will promote (get the word out).
- Choose refreshments and other hospitality needs. (Suggestions are coffee and simple snacks.)

- Begin praying together for the event and for the women whose stories will be shared. (You should choose three women to share ten minutes each with stories related to your theme.)

Four Months Before Your Event

- Develop and agree on a schedule. (It will be important that women have an opportunity to get to know one another—consider using icebreakers at tables with table hostesses to lead them; it will also be important for there to be a natural segue into the stories women will share. You might consider worship or video to introduce the subject you are discussing.)
- Finalize seating and stage arrangements. (Suggestion is to use round tables in a comfortable setting with women who share sitting on stools or sofas on the stage—you want everyone to be comfortable.)
- Review all materials needed, and if printing materials, set deadline for getting materials ready for print. (Printed materials might include tickets, business card invitations, a program for the evening, and maybe even a take-away like a bookmark or postcard.)
- Enlist women whose stories will be shared. Schedule training for them if needed.
- Continue praying.

Two Months Before Your Event

- Revise schedule if needed.
- Make copies of event schedule available to team members (a list of suggested team members follows).
- Enlist volunteers and schedule volunteer training if needed. (You will want table hostesses, greeters, and maybe women

who will pray over others if you choose to allow a time for that.)

- Talk with women about their stories and encourage them.
- If giving away door prizes, collect and decide how you will give them away.
- Continue praying.

One Month Before Your Event

- Meet with team members to make sure they have their tasks on schedule.
- Get printed materials in hand.
- Talk with a technician about specific needs.
- Place orders for refreshments. (You can either purchase these or have a team of women who will provide them.)
- Make sure promotion is continuing and invite, invite, invite. (Small business cards make great invitations and are relatively inexpensive to print.)

One Week Before Your Event

- Final review of project tasks.
- Schedule an event debriefing no more than two weeks after the event.
- Mobilize follow-up event team and equip with resources (for example, if you are sharing stories related to God healing marriages, be ready with a new small group start that is for couples struggling in their marriage).
- Create setup and tear-down checklists.
- Finalize all door prizes, etc.

• Meet with your team to pray on the day of (or day before) the event.

Team Members for an Event Might Include

Technical team: sound and lighting, stage hands, audio/video recorder, photographer, and production assistant

Hospitality team: greeters, ushers, information booth/product sales (perhaps there are books and resources you might want to make available to your participants), child care, and welcome crew

Logistics: setup/tear-down crew, cleaning, parking, and security

Promotions: printed material assembly, media coordinator, distribution, and communication

Audience materials: event tickets, door prizes, programs

Financial: ticket sales, donations/sponsorships, fund-raising, and purchasing

This information was inspired by a great event planning guide I found online at www.outreach.com/Events/Media/OE_EventPlanning Guide.pdf.

Whatever you do, have fun with this! And watch how God will use this activity to inspire your women to share their stories.

Leighann McCoy is a sought-after speaker and author of the well-received *Spiritual Warfare for Women*. She is the prayer and women's minister at a large Southern Baptist church, where her husband serves as pastor, and has written a number of devotionals and curricula. Leighann has been interviewed on numerous radio shows including *For Faith & Family* and Moody Radio. She lives with her family in Franklin, Tennessee.

More Spiritual Insight for Women

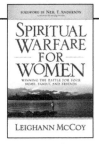
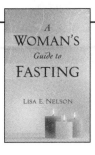